S0-FQY-315

Interior Design Forum

1st Edition

A publication of
Concept Publications, Inc.
A Rockport/Indecs company
P.O. Box 712
Rockport, MA 01966
(508) 546-9401

President: Kenneth Bannon of Concept Publications.
Marketing Director: Kelly Rude
Nitin Kumar of Pro-Index

Book Design & Production:
Blount & Company
Number 12 Station Road
Cranbury, NJ 08512
(609) 655-5785

Cover, Title Pages, Section Pages Design:
Taylor & Browning Design Associates

Printed in Japan by Toppan Printing Company

Linotronic output by Graphic Connexions

ISBN: 0-935603-14-X

Interior Design Forum was published in cooperation with:
Pro-Index, Inc.
4900 Seminary Road
Suite 800
Alexandria, VA 22311
Telephone: (703) 578-6922

Distributed to the book trade and art trade in the U.S. and Canada by:
North Light, an imprint of Writer's Digest Books
1507 Dana Avenue
Cincinnati, OH 45207
Telephone: (513) 984-0717

Distributed to the book trade and art trade throughout the rest of the world by:
Hearst Books International
105 Madison Avenue
New York, NY 10016
Telephone: (212) 481-0355

Other distribution by:
Rockport Publishers
5 Smith Street
Rockport, MA 01966
Telephone: (508) 546-9590
Telex: 5106019284
FAX: (508) 546-7141

INTRODUCTION

You are holding the first edition of INTERIOR DESIGN FORUM—the annual marketplace for buyers of interior design and architectural services. We believe it brings the community of users—the businesses, institutions and individuals who need the skills of the interior architect and designer—an invaluable overview of the range of specialties and skills available to them.

We hope it will also serve as a spur and a mirror; reflecting the very best in contemporary space design and inspiring those who participate in the book and those who purchase it to better solutions; to create even more beautiful and functional environments for their clients.

There truly is something for everyone here. The spaces range from new construction to reconstruction to deconstruction, homes to hospitals, retail stores to restaurants, banks to business offices. The decor styles range from French Provincial through Post Modern.

If you're looking for comfort and efficiency, they abound. If you're looking for eye-catching details, they are here as well.

We have also included the winners of the 1988 honors awards of the New York chapter of the American Institute of Architects. These include the restoration of the Majestic Theater of the Brooklyn Academy of Music and the grand Celeste Bartos Forum belonging to the New York Public Library—proof that, while the past has much to teach the present generation of interior designers, so also can today's practitioners give old spaces a new and vigorous life.

INDEX

CORPORATE

ADVERTISERS

Adaptive Env ronments
621 Huntington Avenue
Boston, MA 02115
(617)739-0038

AIA/New York Chapter
457 Madison Avenue
New York, NY 10022
(212)838-9670

Almasian Associates
167 Washington Street
Sherborn, MA 01770
(508)655-2840

Architectural Interiors Incorporated
2011 I Street NW, Suite 800
Washington, DC 20006
(202)463-6990

Melvin Beacher and Partners Inc.
347 Fifth Avenue
New York, NY 10016
(212)889-6595

Bengtsson International
10704 Hunters Valley Road
Vienna, VA 22180
(703)938-4020

Beyer Blinder Belle
41 East 11th Street
New York, NY 10003
(212)777-7800

Andrew Blackman
121 East 36th Street
New York, NY 10016
(212)683-4884

Kenneth Blaustein + Associates Design
41 Union Square West
Suite 1428
New York, NY 10003
(212)206-7506

Bonsignore Brignati & Mazzotta
275 Seventh Avenue
New York, NY 10001
(212)633-1400

Mark Borchelt
Studio D 4938-D Eisenhower Avenue
Alexandria, VA 22304
(703)751 -2533

Samuel Botero
150 East 58th Street
23rd Floor
New York, NY 10155
(212)935-5155

Bromley Jacobsen
242 West 27th Street
New York, NY 10001
(212)620-4250

Buttrick White & Burtis
475 10th Avenue
7th Floor
New York, NY 10018
(212)967-3333

Rafaell Cabrera International
246 West End Avenue
Suite 2B
New York, NY 10023
(212)787-3851

Cannon
304 East 45th Street
New York, NY 10017
(212)370-0354

Casals • Evans Design Group, Ltd.
225 Lafayette St.
New York, NY 10012
(212)431-0616

Chandler Cudlipp Associates, Inc.
201 E 57th Street
New York, NY 10022
(212)758-0700

Chapman & Biber
422 Morris Avenue
Summit, NJ 07901
(201)273-8877

Alex Chapman
49 Spadina Avene
Suite 507
Toronto, ONT M5V 2J1
(416)597-1576

Tony Chi & Associates
611 Broadway
Suite 724
New York, NY 10012
(212)353-8860

James D'Auria Associates Architects
12 West 27th Street
New York, NY 10001
(212)725-5660

Charles Damga Design
812 Broadway, 2nd Floor
New York, NY 10003
(212)533-8555

DBI
1325 Massachusetts Ave, NW
Suite 700
Washington, DC 20005
(202)393-4500

Der Scutt Architect
44 West 28th Street
New York, NY 10001
(212)725-2300

DeStefano Studios Inc.
34 Commerce Way
Woburn, MA 01801
(617)935-5200

Donghia Associates Inc.
315 East 62 Street
New York, NY 10021
(212)486-1100

Dorcas Design Ltd.
27 East 13th Street
New York, NY 10003
(212)929-3691

DPID, Inc.
One Union Square West
Suite 609
New York, NY 10003
(212)206-6792

DuPont Co.
Fibers Dept.
Walnut Run Building
Wilmington, DE 19880-0722

Environmental Space Planning
14 East 33rd Street
12th Floor
New York, NY 10016
(212)683-2490

Farrell & Greenholz
Design Associates
210 Fifth Ave.
New York, NY 10010
(212)689-5326

Carol Fippin Inc.
83 Newbury Street
Boston, MA 02116
(617)267-8900

Fitzpatrick Design Group Inc.
2109 Broadway
Suite 203
New York, NY 10023
(212)580-5842

Freidin Bolcek Associates, Ltd.
62 West 45th Street
New York, NY 10036
(212)719-1667

Alan Gaynor & Company
434 Broadway
New York, NY 10013
(212)334-0900

Gensler & Associates Architects
One Rockefeller Center, Suite 500
New York, NY 10020
(212)581-9600

Gilpin Gallery
1 Prince Street
Olde Towne
Alexandria, VA 22314
(703)836-0110

GN Associates
595 Madison Avenue
Suite 1406
New York, NY 10022
(212)935-2900

Guenter Roesler Associates Inc.
286 Congress Street
Boston, MA 02210
(617)426-4910

Haines Lundberg Waehler
115 Fifth Avenue
New York, NY 10003
(212)353-4600

Hambrecht Terrell International
860 Broadway
New York, NY 10003
(212)254-1229

Thomas Hauser Designs Ltd.
415 West 55th Street
New York, NY 10019
(212)969-9450

Haverson-Rockwell Architects
18 West 27th Street
4th Floor
New York, NY 10001
(212)889-4182

Margaret Helfand Architects
32 East 38th Street
New York, NY 10016
(212)779-7260

Hellmuth, Obata & Kassabaum
1831 Chestnut Street
St. Louis, MO 63103
(314)421-2000

Hilgenhurst Associates Inc.
300 Massachusetts Avenue
Boston, MA 02115
(617)536-8818

Stephen Roberts Holt Associates
13 Central Street
Manchester, MA 01944
(508)526-1281

Innova Architecture
10801 Main Street
Suite 100
Fairfax, VA 22030
(703)352-4321

Jacobs & Pratt
270 Lafayette Street
New York, NY 10012
(212)226-3994

Kean College of New Jersey
Morris Avenue
Union, NJ 07083
(201)527-2307

Norma King Design Inc.
114 A Sackville Street
Toronto, Ontario M5A 3E7
(416)862-9180

KMR Design Group Inc.
27 East 63rd Street
New York, NY 10021
(212)371-7580

Sam Lopata Inc.
27 West 20th Street
New York, NY 10011
(212)691-7924

JP Maggio Design Associates Inc.
561 Broadway
New York, NY 10012
(212)925-1811

David Lloyd Maron
130 Madison Avenue
New York, NY 10016
(212)889-1480

Milliken Design Center
P.O. Box 2956
LaGrange, GA 30241
(800)241-2327

Milo Kleinberg Design Associates
11 East 26th Street
New York, NY 10010
(212)532-9800

Charles Morris Mount Inc.
104 West 27th Street
New York, NY 10001
(212)807-0800

Newbold Schkufza Design Associates
270 Lafayette Street
New York, NY 10012
(212)334-0909

Nobutaka Ashihara Associates
37 Murray Street
New York, NY 10007
(212)233-1783

Nordstrom Design Group
131 East 29th Street
New York, NY 10016
(212)889-1712

The Olson Group Inc.
25 West 36th Street
New York, NY 10018
(212)239-3636

Owen & Mandolfo
192 Lexington Ave.
New York, NY 10016
(212)686-4576

Papadatos Moudis Associates, PC
305 East 46th Street
New York, NY 10017
(212)308-2500

Parsons School of Design
66 Fifth Avenue
New York, NY 10011
(212)741-8955

Charles Patten Architects
1123 Broadway
New York, NY 10010
(212)929-0338

Perkins Geddis Eastman
437 Fifth Avenue
New York, NY 10016
(212)889-1720

Point of View
Jeffrey W. Curcio
3520 South Sixth Street
Arlington, VA 22204
(703)920-7472

Pratt Institute
200 Willoughby Avenue
Brooklyn, NY 11205
(718)636-3600

Professional Office
Design Magazine
111 Eighth Avenue
New York, NY 10011
(212)463-5800

Rivkin/Weisman PC
141 Fifth Avenue
New York, NY 10010
(212)473-6900

Rogers, Burgun, Shahine
and Deschler, Inc.
215 Park Avenue South
New York, NY 10003
(212)614-0788

Ryan Gibson Bauer Kornblath
One Arin Park
1715 State Highway 35
Middletown, NJ 07748
(201)615-0100

John Saladino
305 East 63rd Street
New York, NY 10021
(212)752-2440

SCR Design
1114 First Avenue
8th Floor
New York, NY 10021
(212)421-3500

Sheridan, Behm, Eustice &
Associates Architecture
3440 Fairfax Drive
Arlington, VA 22201
(703)525-0270

SITE
65 Bleeker Street
New York, NY 10012
(212)254-8300

Skyline Architects and Designers
9 West 19th Street
New York, NY 10011
(212)691-0801

Sultan Blaustein Associates
Design Group
41 Union Square West
Suite 307
New York, NY 10003
(212)206-7506
(212)807-1344

Suma Inc. Design Consultants
236 West 27th Street
New York, NY 10001
(212)807-9590

Swanke Hayden Connell Architects
400 Park Avenue
New York, NY 10022
(212)826-1880

Taylor Clark Architects, Inc.
149 Fifth Avenue
New York, NY 10010
(212)460-8840

Thibeault Design, Inc.
520 Harrison Avenue
Boston, MA 02118
(617)350-0389

Craig Toftey & Associates
45 Middle Street
Gloucester, MA 01930
(508)283-4494

TsAO and McKown
41 East 42nd Street
New York, NY 10017
(212)697-0980

Tucci, Segrete, and Rosen
440 9th Avenue
New York, NY 10001
(212)629-3900

Valerian Rybar & Daigre Design Corp.
601 Madison Avenue
New York, NY 10022
(212)752-1861

Versaille, Inc.
7101 Wisconsin Avenue
Bethesda, MD
(301)657-3646

Voorsanger & Mills Associates
246 West 38th Street
New York, NY 10018
(212)302-6464

Walker Group/CNI
320 West 13th Street
New York, NY 10014
(212)206-0444

Walz Design
141 Fifth Avenue
New York, NY 10011
(212)477-2211

Weber Design
705 King Street
Alexandria, VA 22314
(703)548-0003

Wool Bureau
360 Lexington Ave.
New York, NY 10017
(212)986-6222

Yabu Pushelberg
359 King Street East
Toronto, ONT M5A 1L1
(416)363-1414

ZB Inc.
227 West 17th Street
New York, NY 10011
(212)242-1991

INTERIOR DESIGN CORPORATE

Architectural Interiors

2011 I Street, NW
Suite 800
Washington, DC 20006
(202) 463-6990

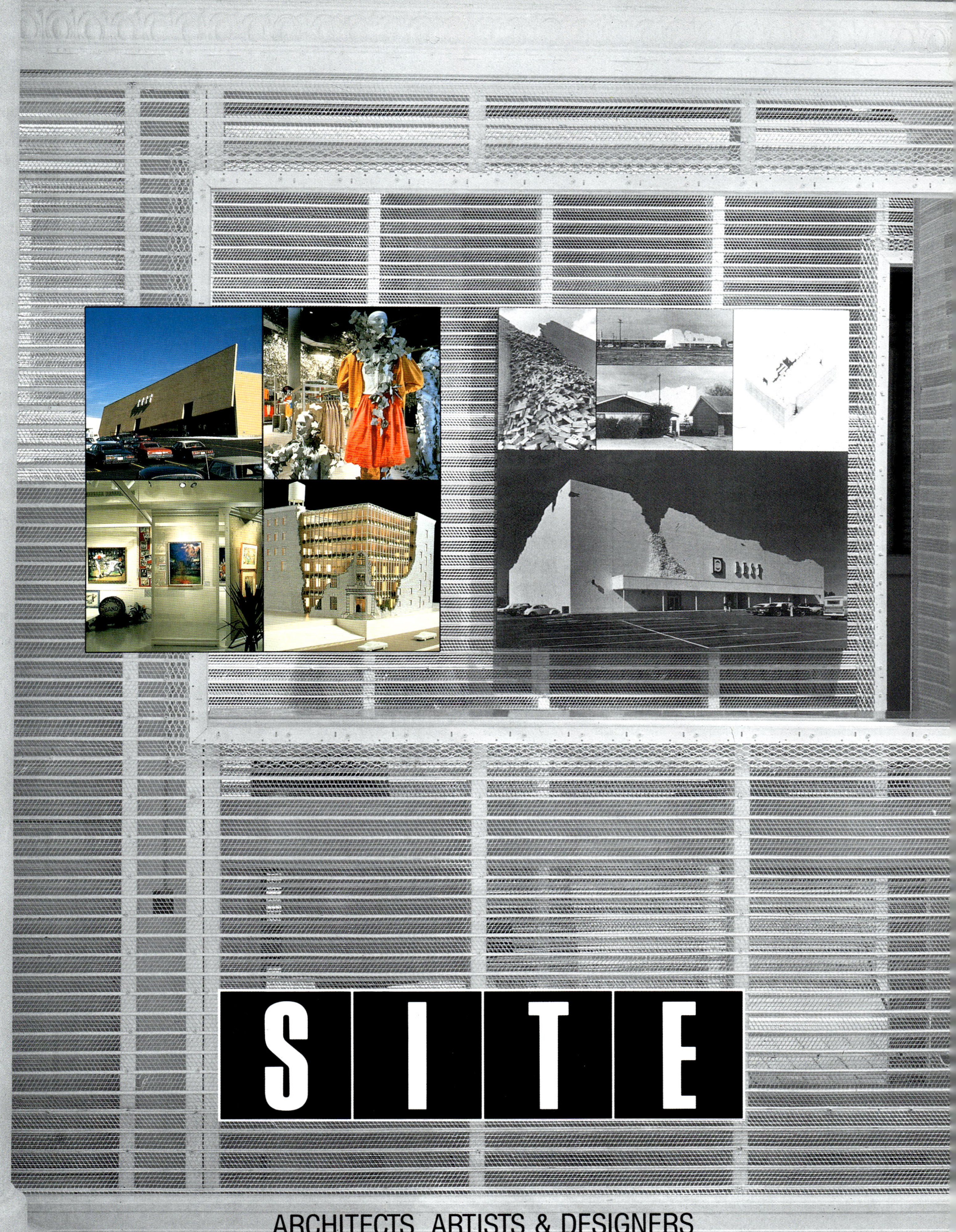

SITE

ARCHITECTS, ARTISTS & DESIGNERS

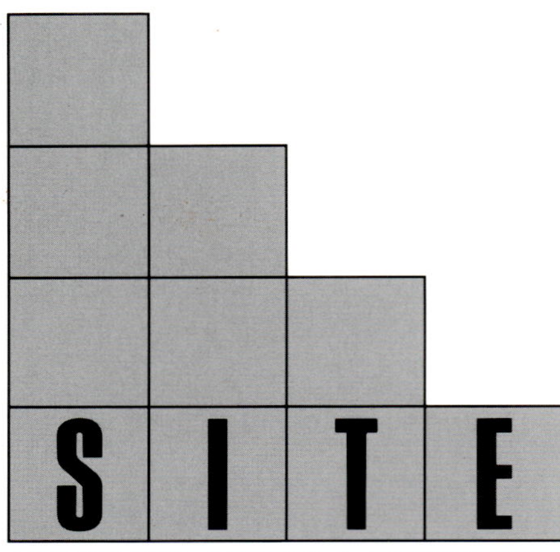

ARCHITECTS, ARTISTS & DESIGNERS

65 Bleecker Street,
New York, NY 10012 USA
Tel 212/254-8300 FAX 212/353-3086

Partners:
Alison Sky
Michelle Stone
Joshua Weinstein
James Wines

SITE is an architectural firm founded in New York City in 1970 for the purpose of serving corporate, civic, and private clients who believe that the structures they build can offer service, economy, and a high level of communication with the public. The group is a unique interdisciplinary team of architects, artists, designers, and technicians dedicated to the creation of buildings, interiors, and public spaces of enduring artistic value.

SITE believes that one of the most important functions of architecture is communication. Without compromising practicality or budget, SITE interprets buildings as the ultimate form of public art—one that can make a strong statement about both clients' and users' personal and cultural identities.

The concepts of SITE are based on a philosophical approach called "narrative architecture"; a very different objective from most current design practice. Whereas the traditions of Modern Design have been based on abstract form, SITE's ideas evolve out of social and psychological influences in today's urban and suburban environments. This means that a structure's facade, interior, and surrounding areas can serve as much more than a composition of volumes, spaces, and materials; they can also deliver compelling narrative messages. The foundation for this direction is rooted in those periods of history—for example, Fourteenth Century Italy—when the building arts told stories as rich and varied as those of a play or a novel.

In developing a project, SITE's creative process includes extensive research and analysis; but, most importantly, it requires a continuous, interactive, collaboration with the client. Final concepts and their realization are always the product of dynamic teamwork. At every stage of design and construction, SITE principals are involved to ensure esthetic control, scheduling, and budget management.

During the past two decades, SITE has built architecture and public spaces throughout the United States and abroad. As a result of the high profile imagery and profitable economic returns of the projects, clients have received international recognition in the art, architecture, business, and popular press of twenty-two countries. In addition, SITE's work has been the subject of fifty museum and private gallery exhibitions in the USA, Europe, and Japan.

Commenting on public indifference to so many contemporary buildings and interiors, social/architectural critic Stephen Kurtz has summarized this crisis of communication as follows: "The processes of building—from those that produce its elements to those it shelters as a completed edifice—are such that it is impossible for human beings to derive satisfaction from them. To the extent that the final product reflects these processes, it reflects that alienation as well." In an endeavor to offer alternatives to this problem, SITE's narrative architecture responds to ideas and issues of the present-day world, anticipates the future, and converts standard construction technology into memorable visual art.

Cutler Ridge Showroom 1979

Andreas Sterzing

Allsteel Showroom 1988

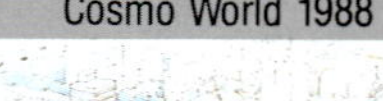

Color photographs on front cover,
clockwise from upper left:
Tilt Showroom 1978
WilliWear Store - 5th Avenue 1988
Paz Building 1984
Museum of the Borough of
Brooklyn 1986

Black & white large photograph
on front cover:
Interior view of the SITE offices,
located in Louis Sullivan's Bayard
Building in New York City

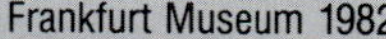

Frankfurt Museum 1982

Indeterminate Facade 1975

Four Continents Bridge 1988

Inside/Outside Showroom 1984

Russell B. Phillips

MacDonald's Restaurant 1984

Andreas Sterzing

WilliWear Men's Showroom 1984

Glen Gery – Brickwork Design Center 1985

Forest Building 1980

Andreas Sterzing

SWATCH Nantucket 1987

Theatre for the New City 1989

Bedford House 1982

Kharen Hill

HIGHWAY 86 PROCESSIONAL – EXPO 86
Vancouver, Canada

This project was a winning competition entry for Canada's Expo 86, celebrating transportation technology since 1940. The public space was a centerpiece of the exposition, uniting two major roadway viaducts, a pedestrian promenade, and the Vancouver harbor. Highway 86 was built of steel and concrete as an undulating, four-lane highway and encrusted with a high density of grey monochromed transport vehicles. The surface of this artery was an "open pavilion" composed of cars, boats, motorcycles, space capsules, lunar rovers, airplanes, bicycles, and other objects of mobility—inviting a visual and participatory response.

Andreas Sterzing

THE LAURIE MALLET HOUSE – 1985
New York, NY

This private residence was designed for a professional woman, of French background, who wanted to expand the space and retain the character of her 1820s Greenwich Village townhouse. The expansion was accomplished by an innovative, partially underground, room constructed under the rear garden. The respect for history involved a layering of information from the past. A number of artifacts from the 1800s—bookcases, fireplaces, doors, mouldings, plus some objects with French references—were converted to ghosted memories which both emerge from and disappear into the walls of the interior and garden.

PERSHING SQUARE – 1989
Los Angeles, CA

Designed for construction in 1989, this major public space was a winning competition entry for the redevelopment of Los Angeles' oldest downtown park. The concept is based on the entire city when viewed from the air—with its mountainous regions surrounding the grid pattern of the urban center—and represents a visual and participatory microcosm of this topography, including all of its regional vegetation and cultural influences. Accommodating an underground parking facility, the carpet-like park and its undulating surfaces hide the unsightly automobile ramps, shelter a restaurant and theatre, and provide a chess game of human activity.

HIGHRISE OF HOMES

This proposal is for a multiple dwelling composed of fifteen to twenty stories, to be constructed in a major urban center. A steel and concrete matrix supports a vertical community of private homes, clustered into village-like communities on each floor. Since highrise residents so often experience a loss of identity in standard housing developments, the purpose of this concept is to provide the option of personalized facades and garden space. In this way, the Highrise of Homes functions as the collective biography of its inhabitants and as a revelation of their individuality expressed in the cityscape.

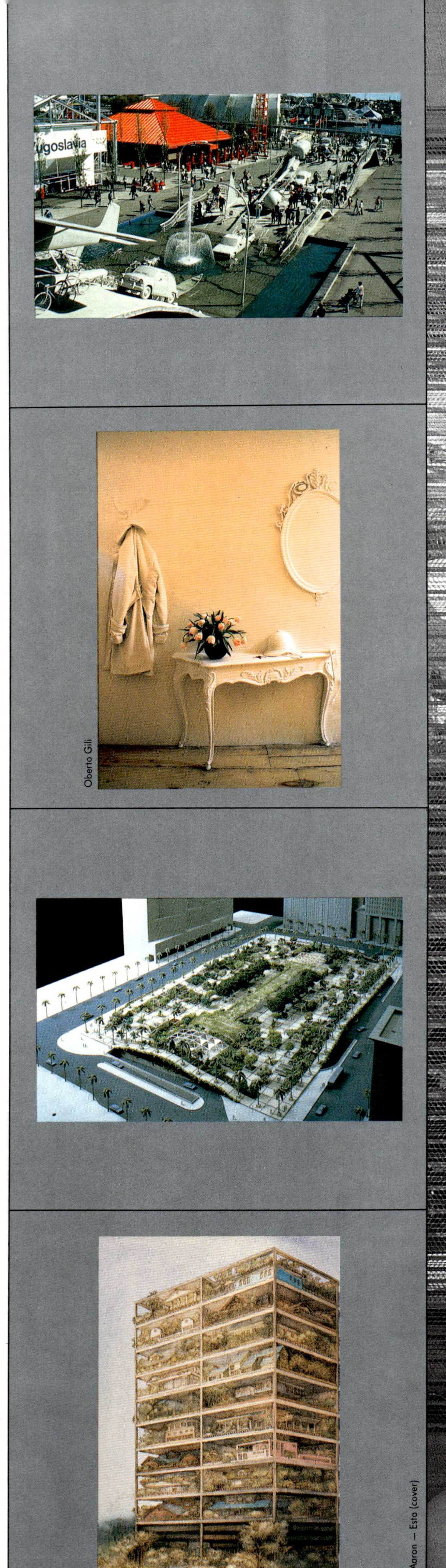

Oberto Gili

Peter Aaron — Esto (cover)

SITE

Brochure Design By Alisa Rashish

Interior Design is the discipline of aesthetics but, more importantly incorporates function, productivity, growth and cost effectiveness.

We at Melvin Beacher & Partners are committed to that discipline.

Melvin Beacher & Partners Inc., 347 Fifth Avenue, NY, NY 10016, 212-889-6595

BONSIGNORE BRIGNATI & MAZZOTTA, P.C. ARCHITECTS

275 SEVENTH AVENUE, NEW YORK, N.Y. 10001 212 633-1400

BONSIGNORE BRIGNATI & MAZZOTTA, P.C. ARCHITECTS 275 SEVENTH AVENUE, NEW YORK, N.Y. 10001 212 633-1400

Photo: Tim Street Porter

Photo: Jeff Goldberg/Esto

BUTTRICK WHITE & BURTIS ARCHITECTS 475 TENTH AVENUE NEW YORK NEW YORK 10018 TEL: 212.967.3333

Impressive interior design begins with impressive credentials

CANNON

Architects
Engineers
Planners
Interior Designers

304 East 45th Street
New York, NY 10017
212/370-0354

Boston
Buffalo
New York
St. Louis
Washington

CASALS • EVANS DESIGN GROUP, LTD. 225 Lafayette St., N.Y., N.Y. (212)431•0616

Chandler Cudlipp Associates, Inc., formed in 1955, is a New York based multi-faceted design firm. The company is responsible for many interior design projects throughout the United States and Europe. Range of projects includes corporate offices, banks, university buildings, hotels and executive conference centers.

CCA Architects, P.C. is an architectural firm engaged in new construction and renovation projects.

CHANDLER CUDLIPP ASSOCIATES, INC.
CCA ARCHITECTS, P.C.
201 EAST 57th ST NEW YORK N Y 10022 212-758-0700

Resort
Austin, Texas

Conference Center
Scottsdale, Arizona

New York, New York

New York, New York

Pittsburgh, Pennsylvania

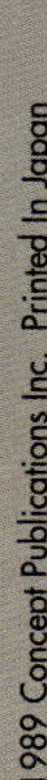

ARCHITECTURE PLANNING INTERIOR DESIGN

422 Morris Avenue Summit, New Jersey 07901 (201) 273-8877

1325
Massachusetts Avenue
N.W.
Suite 700
Washington, DC
20005
(202) 393-4500

8320
Old Courthouse Road
Suite 410
Vienna, VA
22180
(703) 893-3950

At DBI, we design interiors that are good for business.

We put more image, and more performance, into fewer square feet.

Our office plans reflect the smart, efficient operation every client appreciates.

In fact, DBI has created the hardest working offices in Washington.

How do we do it?

The first thing DBI draws is an accurate picture of your company.

We look at current requirements and growth projections. We chart the flow of traffic and communication. We determine how to increase space flexibility.

Then we can draw a business environment that proves better doesn't mean bigger; more efficient doesn't mean more expensive.

When DBI designs office space, it never looks like your company cut corners.

For a hard-working interior, call DBI.

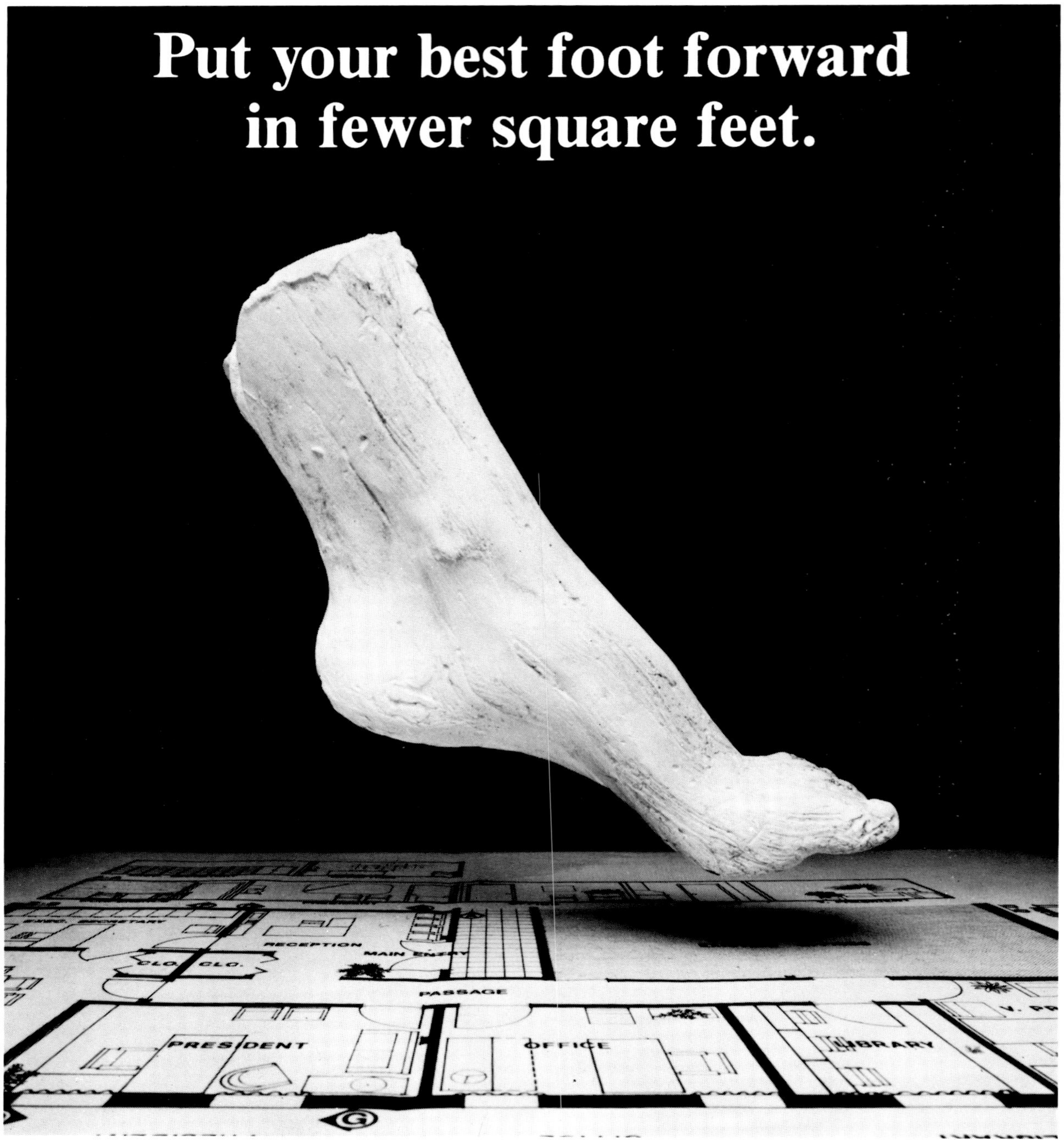

Put your best foot forward in fewer square feet.

LAB CORRIDOR

PERFUMERS CORRIDOR

APPLICATIONS LAB

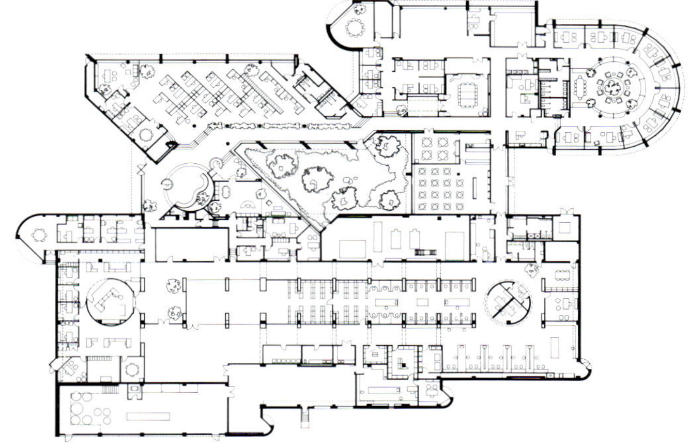

PLAN

ROURE, INC.
TEANECK, NEW JERSEY

This international fragrance company enjoys a variety of interior experiences employing bold use of form, lighting and color. Der Scutt was the building's original designer in 1973 and due to Roure's phenomenal growth, Der Scutt Architect was commissioned in 1981 to completely renovate the interior to allow for further growth.

PRESIDENT'S OFFICE

VICE PRESIDENT'S OFFICE

PERFUMERS CONFERENCE

PERFUMERS SUITE

SALES PLATFORM

PRIVATE DINING ROOM

ROURE, INC.
TEANECK, NEW JERSEY

The design goal was to create interiors that would motivate and inspire the occupants. The client has attributed their continued growth in sales directly to the creative interior design.

Der Scutt Architect

44 West 28th Street New York, New York 10001 212 725 2300 FAX: (212) 481-7094

RECEPTION

PRESIDENT'S OFFICE

EXECUTIVE CORRIDOR

SENIOR VICE PRESIDENT'S OFFICE

ENHANCE FINANCE CO.—CORPORATE OFFICES
NEW YORK CITY

Der Scutt Architect was engaged to provide architectural and interior design for a newly formed financial investment group. The 10,000-square-foot floor at 360 Madison Avenue was to be refurbished using 95% of the existing partitions already in place. The three corner executive offices were reconfigured and enlarged.

A completely new interior design involving painting, carpeting, lighting, ceilings, and other special equipment was provided. A completely new furniture and accessory program was developed. The client mandated a rigid and specific budget, which was respected.

The project was designed in six weeks and construction was completed in three months.

Simple use of accent color and careful attention to lighting contribute to these quiet dignified offices.

CENTRAL CORRIDOR

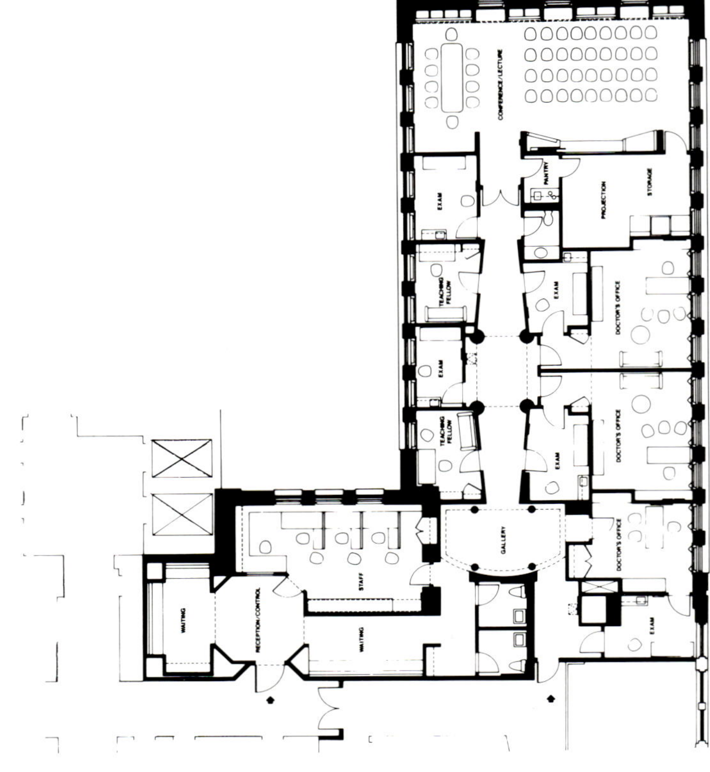

PLAN

RECEPTION

ST. LUKE'S—ROOSEVELT HOSPITAL
HAND SURGERY CLINIC
NEW YORK CITY

Der Scutt Architect was commissioned to space plan and design a hand surgery suite, within a functioning hospital. This facility is for the two most eminent hand surgeons in the United States. It provides facilities for both patient diagnosis and care and a teaching/conference center for the ongoing development and dissemination of techniques pertaining to this unique field.

The suite includes doctors' and exam rooms; resident "fellows" offices; reception/waiting and staff rooms; and a lecture/conference room with state of the art audio-visual and information storage systems. Der Scutt Architect worked closely with the doctors in determining and implementing their requirements. This relationship continued with the Hospital's Administrative Staff, Architects and Consultants.

The primary design goal was to employ the use of form, color and lighting to create an environment distinctly different from the hospital norm.

Der Scutt Architect

44 West 28th Street New York, New York 10001 212 725 2300 FAX: (212) 481-7094

LOBBY FROM ENTRANCE

ELEVATOR HALL

ATRIUM

LOBBY

100 FAIRFIELD AVENUE
BRIDGEPORT, CONNECTICUT

The developer's goal was to transform the former Justice Building on Main Street into a prestigious office complex for legal and accounting firms. The building was upgraded to attract first-class commercial office tenants and to initiate the revitalization of the center of Bridgeport.

The original one-story entrance was replaced with a two-story high lobby with trees, marble and lighting. An existing interior four-story atrium was refurbished with a new skylight to highlight the new atrium office lobbies. Form, color, and rich materials embellish the ambience.

Der Scutt Architect

44 West 28th Street New York, New York 10001 212 725 2300 FAX: (212) 481-7094

PRESIDENT'S OFFICE

BANKERS PLATFORM

PRESIDENT'S SUITE

INTERNATIONAL RECEPTION

CONFERENCE ROOM

EXECUTIVE RECEPTION

THE HONGKONG AND SHANGHAI BANKING CORP.
CORPORATE HEADQUARTERS, NEW YORK CITY

The bank requested a traditional ambience with the installation of previously owned furniture.

Der Scutt Architect

44 West 28th Street New York, New York 10001 212 725 2300 FAX: (212) 481-7094

Prior to the establishment of DORCAS DESIGN LTD., Ms. Roehrs designed and participated on the following projects.

WELTON BECKET ASSOCIATES

CORPORATE OFFICES

LEVER BROTHERS
Headquarters, Englewood Cliffs, NJ (published)

ENPRO N.V. Juffali U.S. Headquarters, New York, NY

HOTELS

THE GREAT WALL HOTEL 1007 rooms, Beijing, China
Published in: THE DESIGNER 9-84; DESIGNER WEST 3-84; HOTEL AND RESTAURANT INTERNATIONAL 9-84

BUENA VISTA PALACE HOTEL 1000 rooms
Lake Buena Vista, FL (Disney World)

BUENA VISTA PALACE HOTEL 50,000-sq.-ft. addition
Ballroom, Prefunction Area, (4) Meeting Rooms
Lake Buena Vista, FL (Disney World)

RESTAURANTS

Le FRANCE Specialty Restaurant - GWH, China

ORCHID PAVILION Rooftop Restaurant - GWH, China

SUMMIT Rooftop Lounge - GWH, China

THE SILK ROADS Main Dining Room - GWH, China

PAGODA COURT Atrium Tea Garden - GWH, China

ORIENT EXPRESS Coffee Shop - GWH, China

COSMOS Disco - GWH, China

WYMAN AND CANNAN

EL PRESIDENTE HOTEL
(Graphics-phone system) Mexico City, Mexico

HARPER AND GEORGE

RESTAURANTS

RAINBOW GRILL Rockefeller Plaza, New York, NY

MIAMI MARINA Miami, FL

AIRLINES

AIR FLORIDA CTO'S & Terminal Ticket Counter, Miami, FL

BRANIFF Executive Lounge (addition & renovation), Dallas, TX

CHERMAYEFF AND GEISMAR

EXHIBITS

SMITHSONIAN INSTITUTION "A Nation of Nations"
Washington, D.C., (Received 1977 IDSA Award)

BURLINGTON MILLS "The Mill" Lobby, New York, NY

ALFRED SCHOLZ ASSOCIATED INC.

LIGHTING DESIGN

ANACONDA TOWER Atlantic Richfield Company
Denver, CO. Published in: INTERIOR DESIGN 5-80

U.S. SENATE OFFICE SYSTEMS RESEARCH PROJECT
Washington, D.C.

ICI UNITED STATES

WESTERN SAVINGS BANK

MOBIL OIL

ALEXANDER & ALEXANDER
Stamford, CT

DORCAS
DESIGN
LTD
9 WEST 19TH STREET
FOURTH FLOOR
NEW YORK, NY 10011
212-620-0338

Photo: Scott Francis

Photography: Donald Vascimini

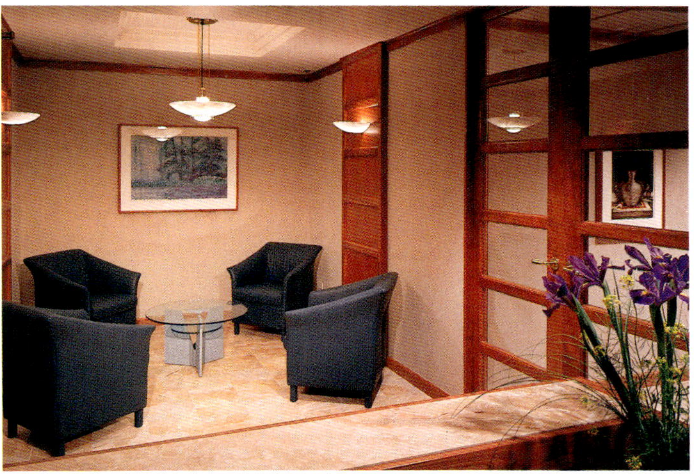

F&G Design Associates, Inc.

Architecture and Interior Design
210 Fifth Avenue, New York, NY 10010
Telephone: 212-689-5326

CAROL FIPPIN INC.

Photos: © 1988 Steve Rosenthal

CAROL FIPPIN INC.

83 NEWBURY STREET
BOSTON
MASSACHUSETTS
02116

617 267-8900

CFI is in a unique position to bring together many diverse design talents and services for architecture, interior planning, and interior design, and has been involved with a variety of private and public projects requiring complete planning and design, administration, programming, construction documents, production services and supervision.

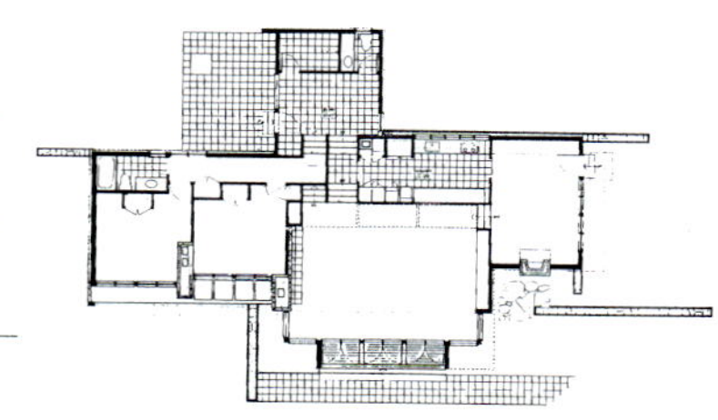

To maintain creativity,
versatility and
imaginative design,
FBA practices
variety...

a beach house
in Southampton,
an archives building
and museum
in Antigua, W.I.,
a weekend house
in upstate New York,
major alterations
to residences in
Scarsdale and
New York City...

... and offices
in a dozen cities
throughout the U.S...

a bank,
investment firm,
publishing company,
communications firm,
real estate company,
lawyers' office...

FBA **Freidin Bolcek Associates, Ltd.**

62 West 45th Street
New York, NY 10036
(212) 719-1667

Jack Freidin, A.I.A.
Ivan A. Bolcek

Architecture Planning InteriorDesign

Architecture, Interior Design, Facilities Management
434 Broadway, New York, NY 10013–2577 212·334·0900

ALAN GAYNOR & COMPANY, P.C.

Architec

ALAN GAYNOR & COMPANY, P.C.

Architecture

Interior Design Forum 1 Printed in Japan

Photo: © Mark Darley Design: Jonathan Wajskol NYC

GN ASSOCIATES

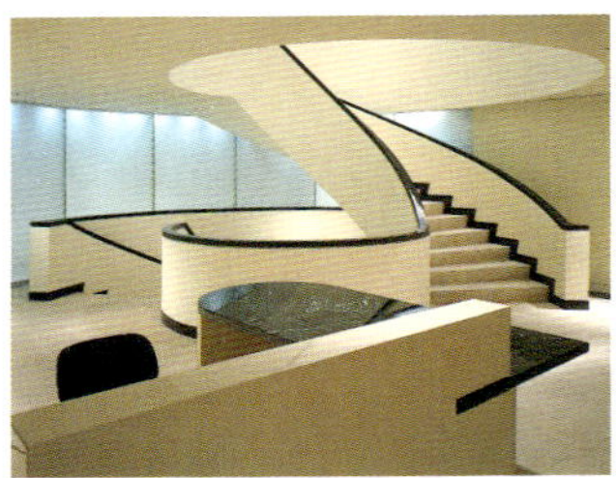

1.

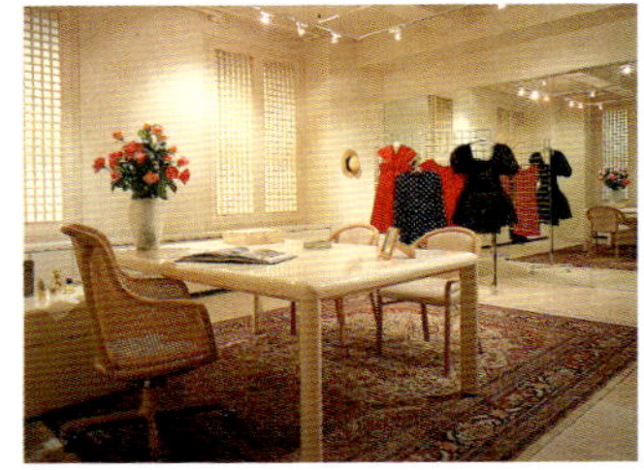

2.

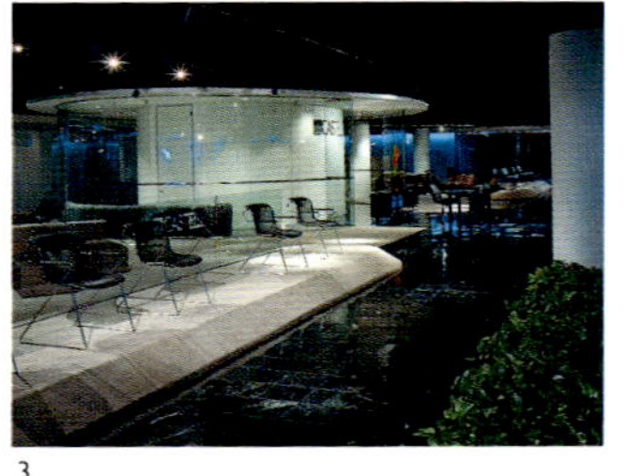

3.

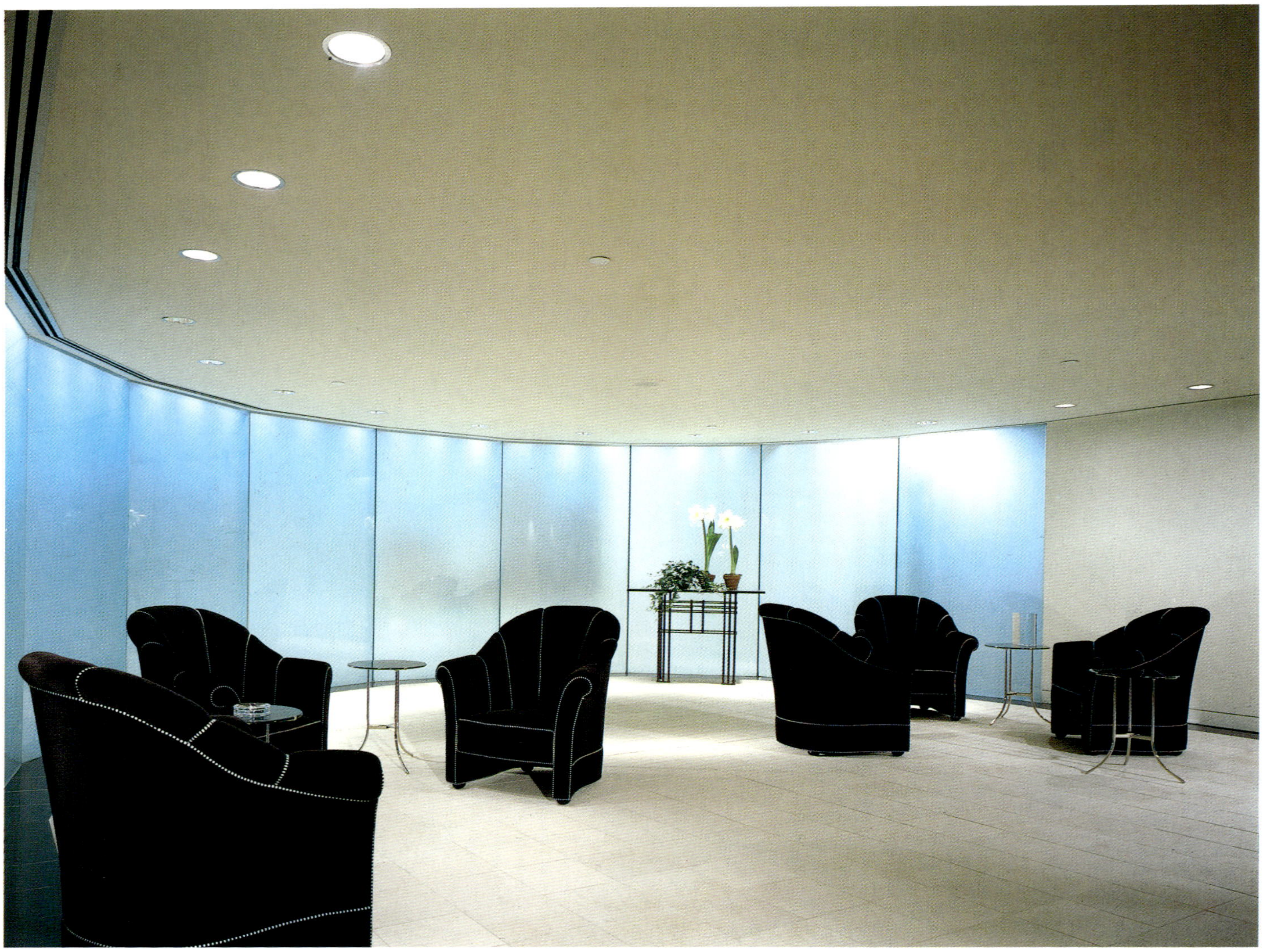

1.

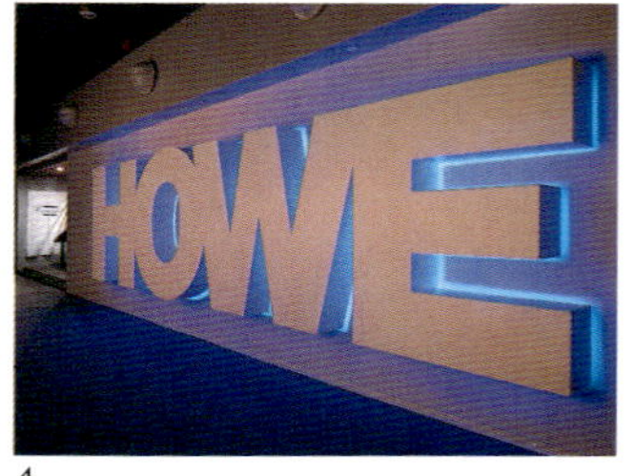

4.

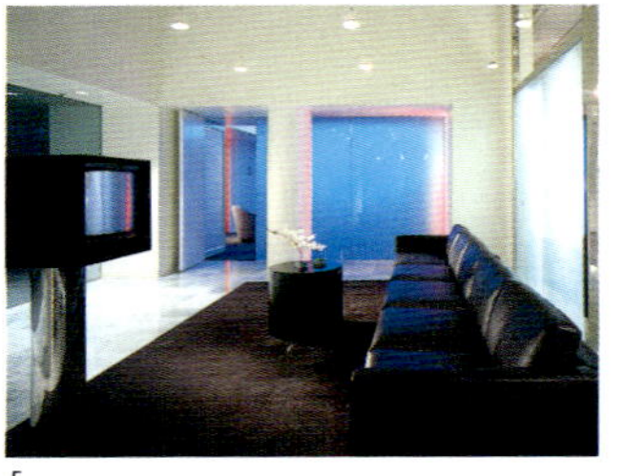

5.

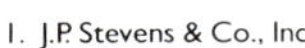

1. J.P. Stevens & Co., Inc.
2. Carolyne Roehm
3. Castelli Furniture, Inc.
4. Howe Furniture
5. Westinghouse Furniture Systems

6.

6.

Interior Planning
Design
Graphics

595 Madison Avenue
New York, New York 10022
212 935-2900

6.

Photography / Durston Saylor

7.

8.

9.

6. Union Trust Bank
   (Signet Bank/Maryland)
7. Sullivan and Worcester
8. General Electric Company
9. Shearson Lehman Hutton, Inc.

286 CONGRESS STREET BOSTON MASSACHUSETTS 02210 617 426-4910

Gensler and Associates/

Architects providing

comprehensive architectural

interior design services

*100 United Nations Plaza,
New York, NY (top photo)*

*Cadwalader, Wickersham & Taft,
New York, NY (bottom photo)*

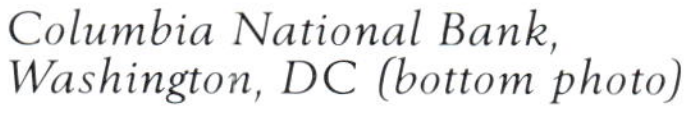

*Covington & Burling,
Washington, DC (top photo)*

*Columbia National Bank,
Washington, DC (bottom photo)*

Gensler and Associates is a full-service architectural firm where excellence in design is measured by how well human needs are balanced with the functional, economic and technical requirements of a space. Aesthetics and image are important, but are only part of a broader-based design solution that must reflect the client's growth patterns, operational methods, and objectives.

Interior Design Magazine has ranked us the top interior design firm for the last eight of nine years and the best managed design firm for the two years of the listing. For the past nine years our professional peers have voted us the firm most respected for design ability.

In light of this significant recognition from the industry, we are continually strengthening our commitment to work with our clients to create environments that exemplify excellence in design and function and facilitate user comfort and efficiency.

Gensler and Associates Architects

One Rockefeller Center, Suite 500
New York, New York 10020
212-581-9600
Margo C. Grant
Managing Principal
Walter A. Hunt, Jr., AIA
Managing Principal

1101 17th Street N.W., Suite 903
Washington, D.C. 20036
202-887-5400
Christopher C. Murray, III, AIA
Managing Principal

Gensler and Associates/Architects also has offices in San Francisco, Denver, Houston, and Los Angeles.

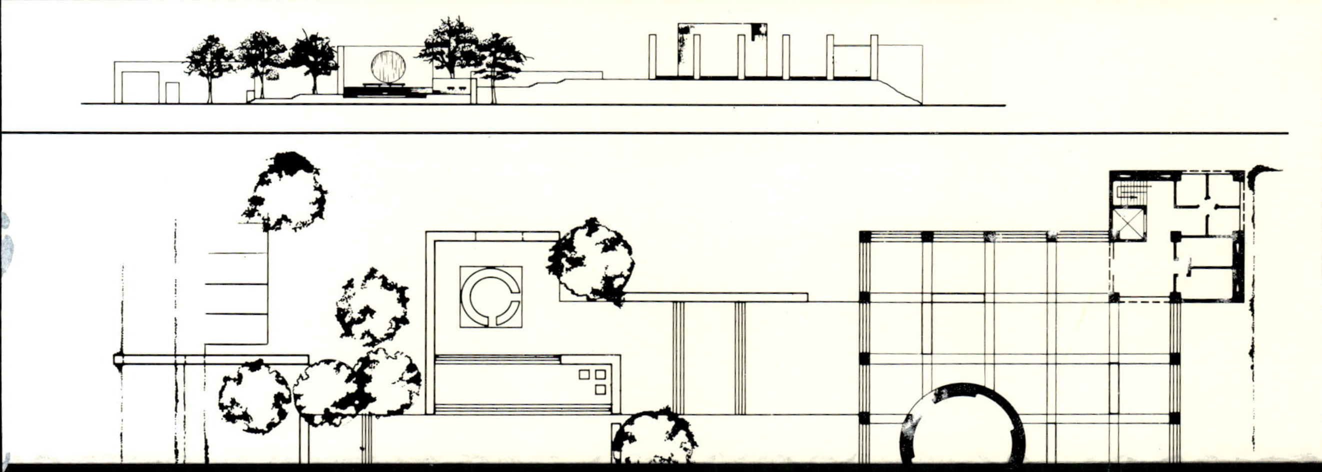

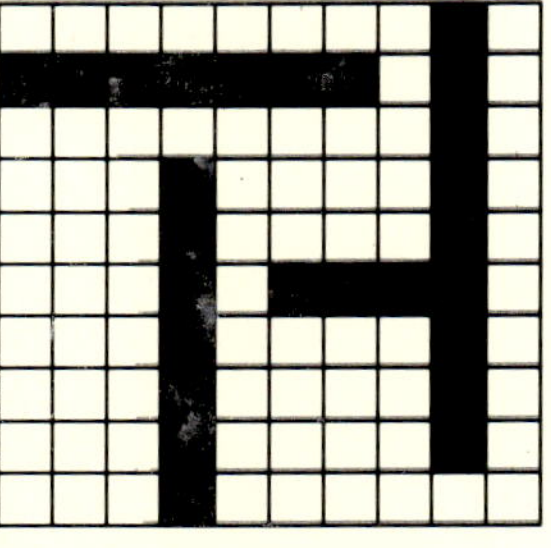

THOMAS HAUSER
DESIGNS LTD

415 WEST 55TH STREET
NEW YORK, N.Y. 10019

PROPOSED MEMORIAL CENTER
NEW JERSEY

ROSEHILL COLUMBARIUM
LINDEN, NEW JERSEY

PHOTOGRAPHY: DENNIS KRUKOWSKI

O'BRIEN RISERVATO SHOWROOM
NEW YORK, NEW YORK

PHOTOGRAPHER: ANDREW APPELL

WATERY SMOOTHNESS OF SAND BLASTED GLASS, BEDS OF DARK SHINY STONES, AND MODELED EARTH COLORED WALLS

DONNA HAIR DESIGN
CHAPPAQUA, NEW YORK

GRAPHIC DESIGN: ROBERT COON
PHOTOGRAPHY: ANDREW APPELL

HILGENHURST

GEORGE FISHER		HILGENHURST ASSOCIATES INCORPORATED
MALCOLM MACKENZIE	ARCHITECTURE	300 MASSACHUSETTS AVENUE
JEFFRY POND	INTERIOR DESIGN	BOSTON, MASSACHUSETTS 02115
LEIGH ROONEY		

Haines Lundberg Waehler
Architects Engineers and Planners
115 Fifth Avenue New York NY 10003

Bozell, Jacobs, Kenyon & Eckhardt

New York, New York

"The historic image was blended with a verve reflective of the agency's services."
—Interiors *magazine, July 1986*

Image-making is the business of advertising, and this 150,000 sq. ft. space for a major agency uses interior design theatrically to create a distinctive identity. The approach is contemporary, but it respects the character of the building's cast iron architecture.

A close integration of interior design, architectural renovation, and engineering was the key to designing this modern office environment that makes a special statement about the importance of image to its occupants.

Before restoration

Photo Credits
Opposite:
Peter Paige
Back:
Top, left: K. Mascheroni
All others: Peter Paige

Haines Lundberg Waehler
Architects Engineers and Planners
115 Fifth Avenue New York NY 10003

Schering-Plough Corporation

Madison, New Jersey

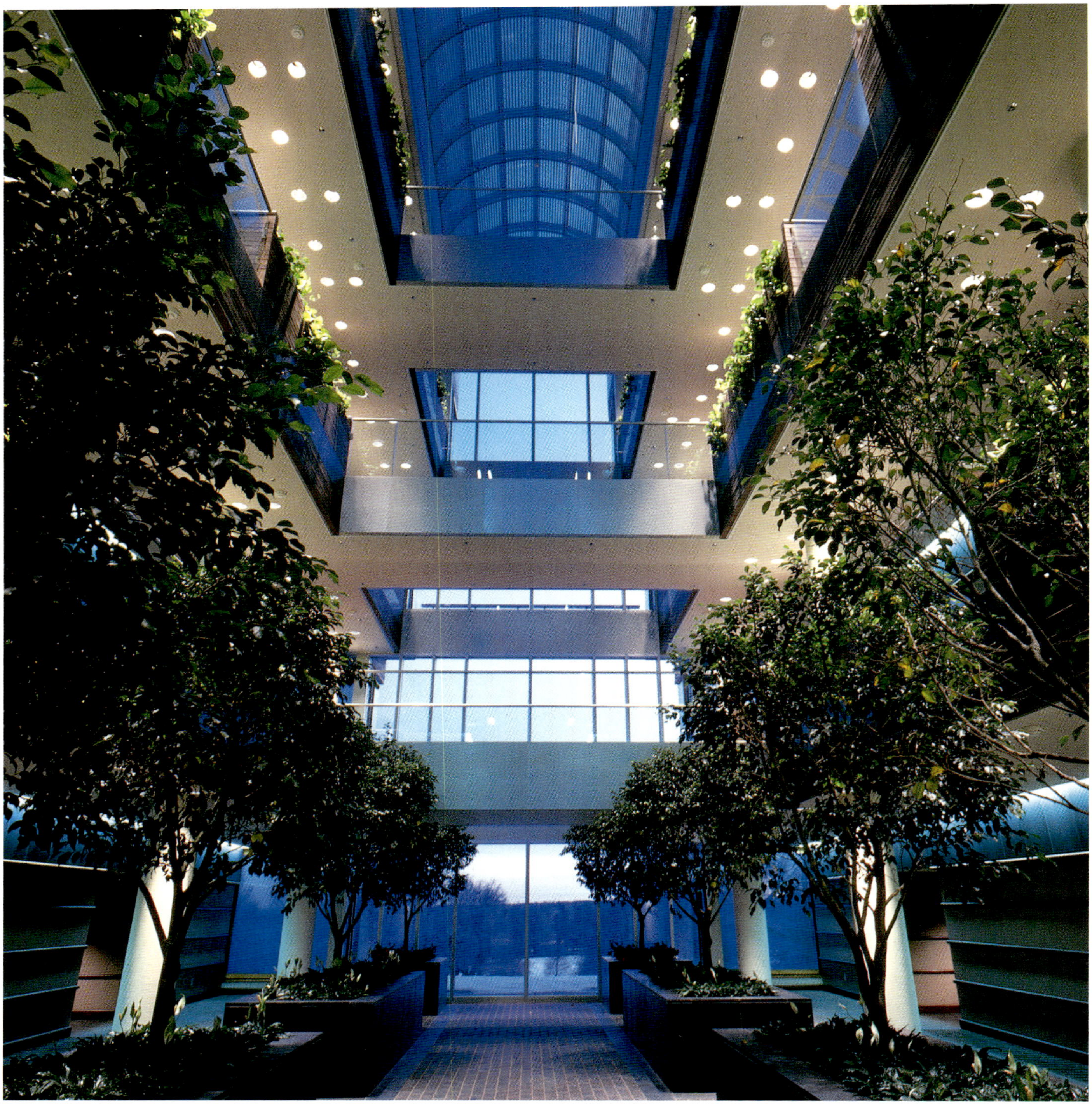

"People were visibly uplifted when they came here,"
—Harold R. Hiser, Jr., Schering-Plough, senior vice president for finance.

Architectural form, warm colors, and natural materials such as wood and granite relate this 150,000 sq. ft. corporate headquarters to its pastoral site. HLW's full resources—from programming and design to landscape architecture and engineering—were called into play in order to create a place that meets this client's aesthetic, environmental, functional, and technological goals.

Photo Credit
George Cserna

Kellogg Company Corporate Headquarters Battle Creek, Michigan

Hellmuth, Obata & Kassabaum (HOK) is a highly diversified professional design services firm whose philosophy is to design "from the inside out . . . to provide space that will enhance the lives of building occupants."

Hellmuth, Obata & Kassabaum

1831 Chestnut Street
St. Louis, Missouri 63103
Telephone: 314 421 2000
Telex: 44 7192 HOK STL

Architecture
Interior design
Facility programming
Graphic design
Engineering
Planning

Emily Morgan Hotel San Antonio, Texas

Price Waterhouse Long Beach, California

Gunster, Yoakley, Criser & Stewart Attorneys at Law West Palm Beach, Florida

The First Boston Corporation Dallas, Texas

HOK has offices in New York, Washington, DC, Tampa, St. Louis, Dallas, Kansas City, San Francisco, Los Angeles, and London.

Stephen Roberts Holt & Associates
13 Central Street   Manchester, Massachusetts 01944
(508) 526-1281

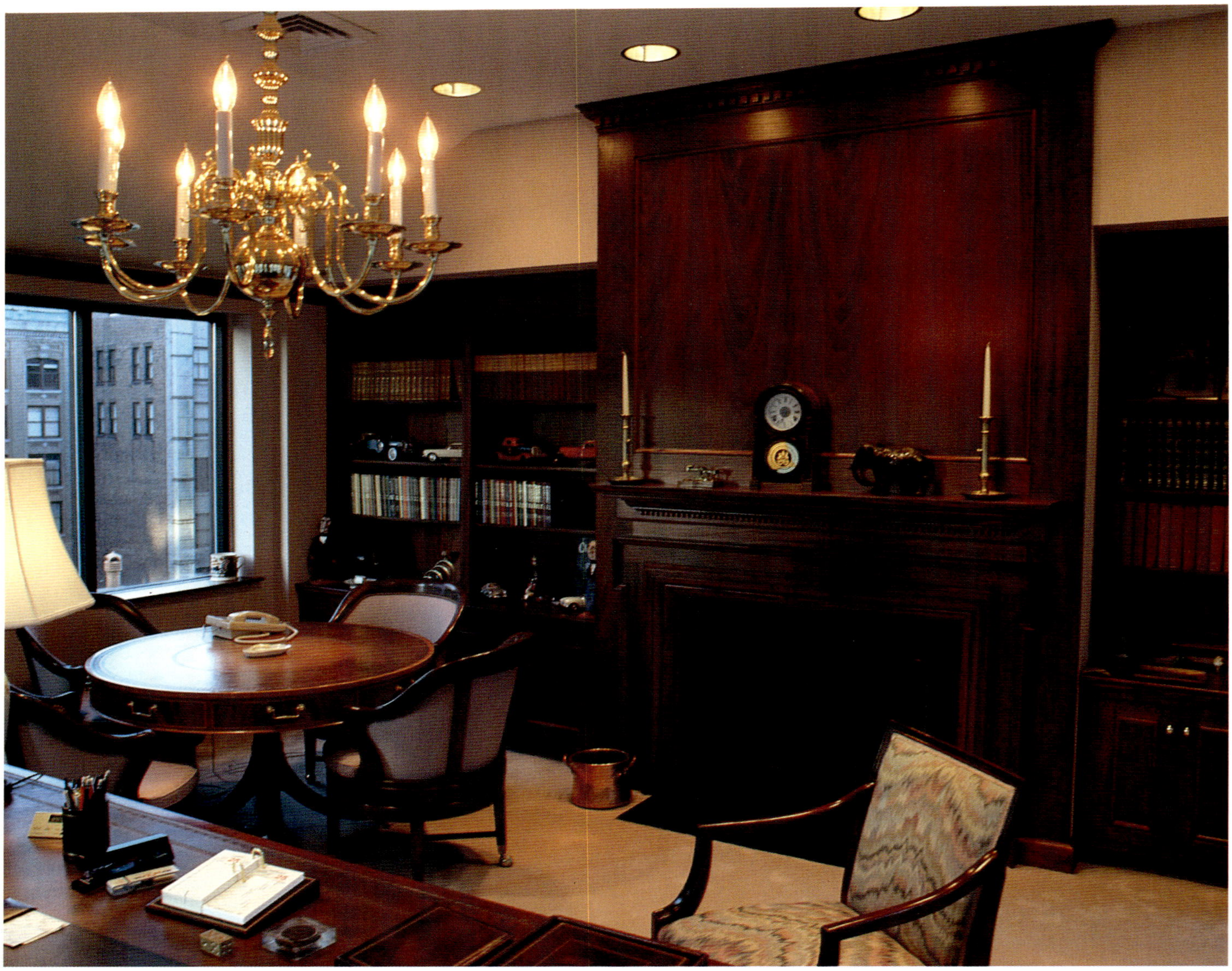

EXECUTIVE OFFICES   CLUBS   LAW/BROKERAGE FIRMS   HOTELS   RESORTS   RESIDENCES

INNOVA

ARCHITECTURE

INNOVA Architecture is a full service, building design and planning firm. We are a results oriented, mid-size organization with an outstanding reputation for quality and timely service.

INNOVA's capabilities and experience are extensive. Over the last 25 years, we have been involved in the design and construction of a wide range of building and project types. Whether it is planning and building design, commercial, residential, educational, institutional or mixed-use development, we can respond to the challenge of every project.

Our extensive experience has given the professionals at INNOVA a thorough understanding of the many aspects of building technology. Our goal is to always meet our clients' needs with good design and sound technical expertise. This is how we have built our reputation for quality architecture.

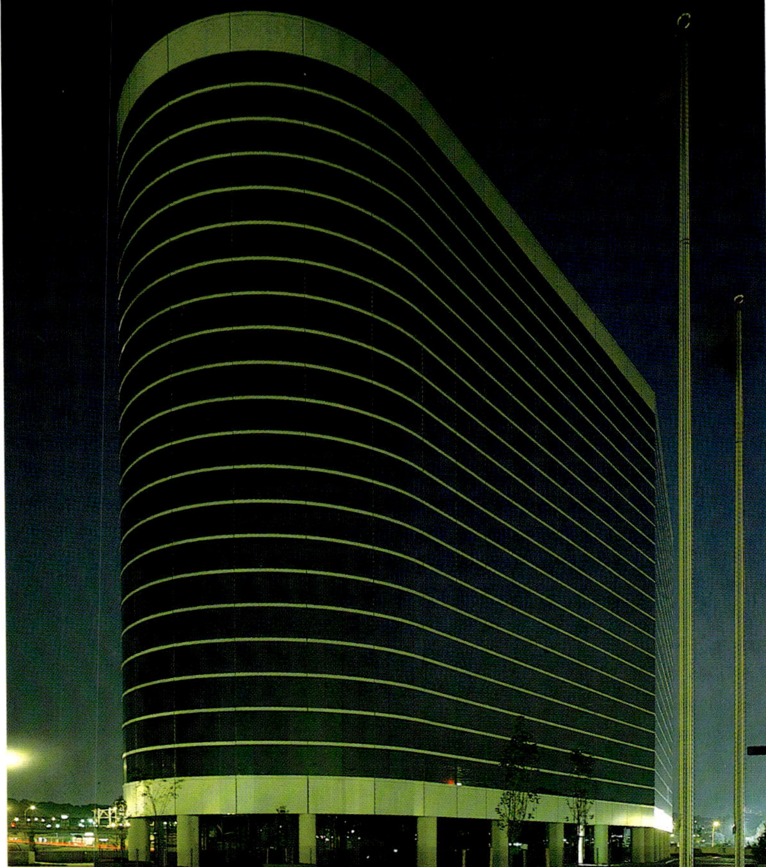

10801 Main Street
Suite 100
Fairfax, Virginia 22030
(703) 352-4321

INNOVA
ARCHITECTURE

maggio
JP MAGGIO DESIGN ASSOCIATES INC. 561 BROADWAY NEW YORK, N.Y. 10012

KMR DESIGN GROUP INC.
27 EAST 63RD STREET
NEW YORK, NEW YORK 10021

FULL SERVICE COMMERCIAL & RESIDENTIAL DESIGN
PREVIOUS HEXTER AWARD WINNER

1 2 3 7 6 4 5

1. C.E.O. CORPORATE OFFICE PHOTO: JOHN HALL
2. THE RITZ NYC THEATER PHOTO: PETER PAIGE
3. EXECUTIVE OFFICE ABC NEWS PHOTO: JOHN HALL
4. NEW YORK CITY CORPORATE APARTMENT PHOTO: ROBERT BERNARD
5. NEW YORK CITY BOUTIQUE PHOTO: SCOTT FRANCIS
6. YOUNG MEN'S PHILANTHROPIC LEAGUE BAR/DINING ROOM PHOTO: SCOTT FRANCIS
7. YOUNG MEN'S PHILANTHROPIC LEAGUE RECEPTION AREA PHOTO: SCOTT FRANCIS

KAREN M. ROSEN, PRESIDENT

Global Union Bank

Global Union Bank

Bertlyn Inc.

Le Jacq Publishing

Quotron Systems

Since 1959, an innovator in New York of creative office planning and design, construction management and real estate consulting.

MILO KLEINBERG
DESIGN ASSOCIATES, INC.

11 EAST 26TH STREET
NEW YORK, NY 10010
(212) 532-9800

OUR PROFESSIONAL SERVICES INCLUDE

* PROJECT MANAGEMENT
* PROGRAMMING
* FINANCIAL ANALYSIS
* FURNITURE INVENTORY
* FEASIBILITY STUDIES
* SPACE PLANNING
* CONCEPT DEVELOPMENT
* DESIGN
* FURNITURE SPECIFICATION
* CONSTRUCTION DOCUMENTATION
* COORDINATION
* BUDGETING
* SCHEDULING
* FOLLOW-UP

OLSON GROUP, INC.
PROGRAM MANAGEMENT, INTERIORS

TWENTY-FIVE WEST THIRTY SIXTH STREET, NEW YORK, NEW YORK 10018 • (212) 239-3636

Owen & Mandolfo is a full service interior design firm specializing in the design of corporate office space. The company has extensive experience in facilities planning and in financial and retail design.

Owen & Mandolfo, Inc. 192 Lexington Avenue New York, New York 10016 (212) 686-4576 Overseas Offices: Paris, France Munich, Germany

ARCHITECTURE • PLANNING • INTERIORS • RESTORATIONS

BRIDGEWATER PLAZA II
BRIDGEWATER, NEW JERSEY

Architects/Planners
PAPADATOS MOUDIS ASSOCIATES P.C.
305 EAST 46TH STREET • NEW YORK, N.Y. 10017 • 212/308-2500

Interior Design Forum © PAPADATOS MOUDIS ASSOCIATES P.C./1989

HERZOG HEINE GEDULD
NEW YORK CITY

APPLE BANK
NEW YORK CITY

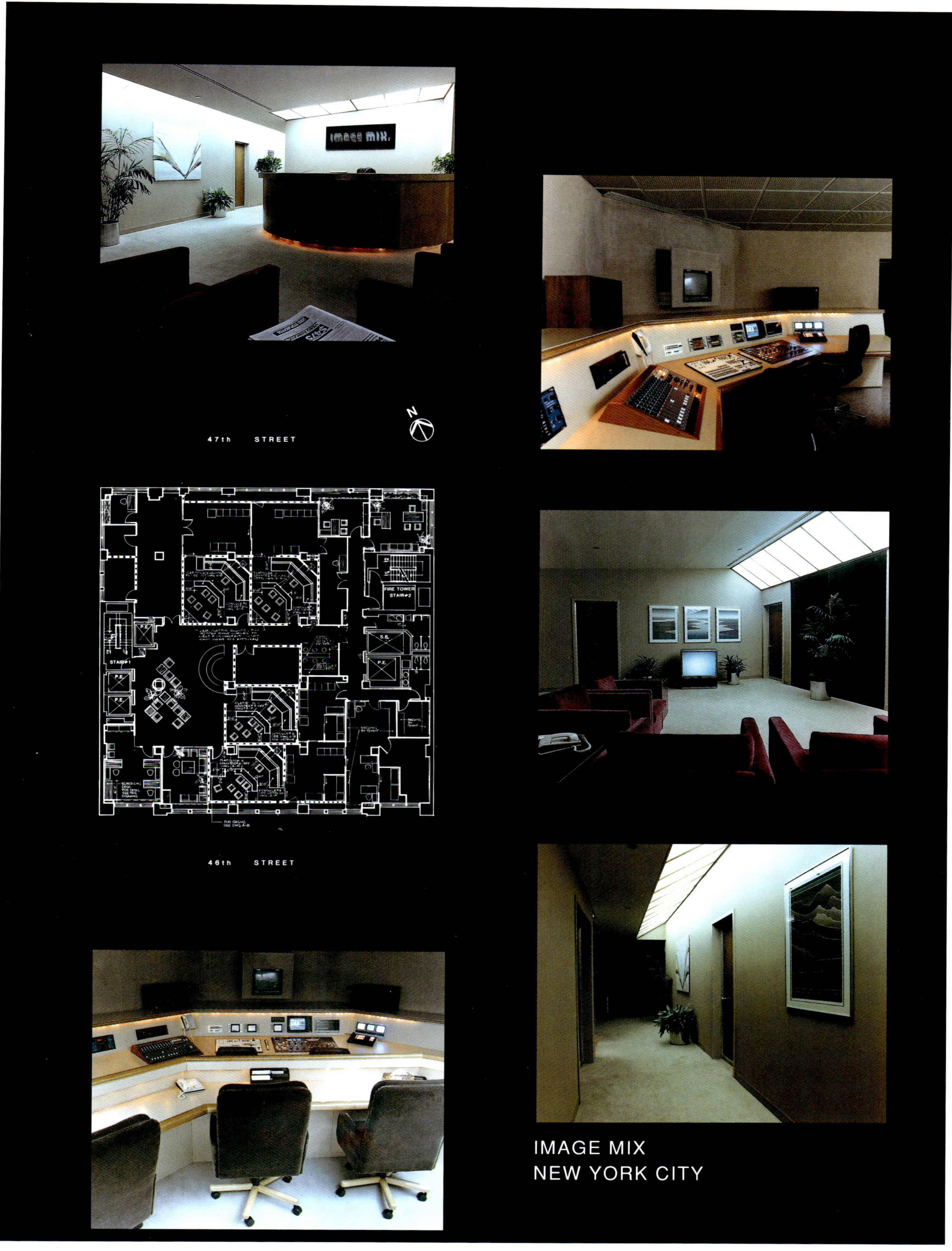

IMAGE MIX
NEW YORK CITY

ST. GEORGE BASILICA — NORWALK, CONNECTICUT

DnC America Banking Corporation

Scali McCabe Sloves Advertising

The W.B. Wood Company

Photography by Durston Saylor

PERKINS GEDDIS EASTMAN ARCHITECTS

Shea & Gould II

Shea & Gould I

Perkins Geddis Eastman has designed a wide variety of corporate, professional office and institutional interiors. Our goal is to create a unique environment tailored to the specific needs and aspirations of each client. All projects are managed by one of the principals leading an integrated team of architects and interior designers who insure a comprehensive approach to the entire design process.

The New York Foundling Hospital

Perkins
Geddis
Eastman

Architects

437 Fifth Avenue New York, New York 10016 212.889 1720

At Ryan Gibson Bauer Kornblath, PA
Interior Architecture is a Creative Process

© George Cserna

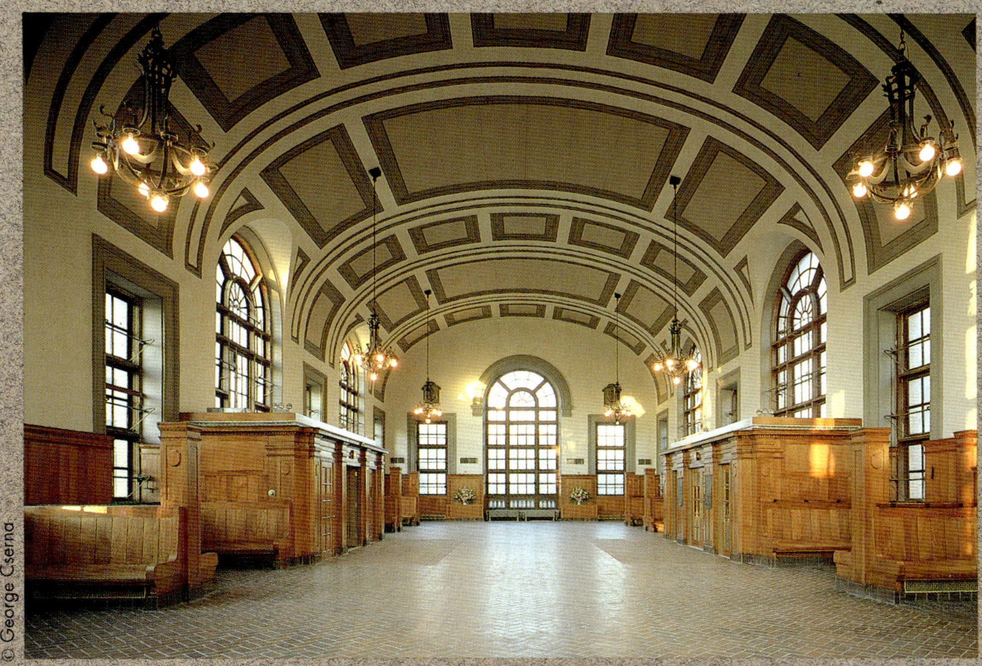

A process in which
we and our clients
work together
as a team...

© George Cserna

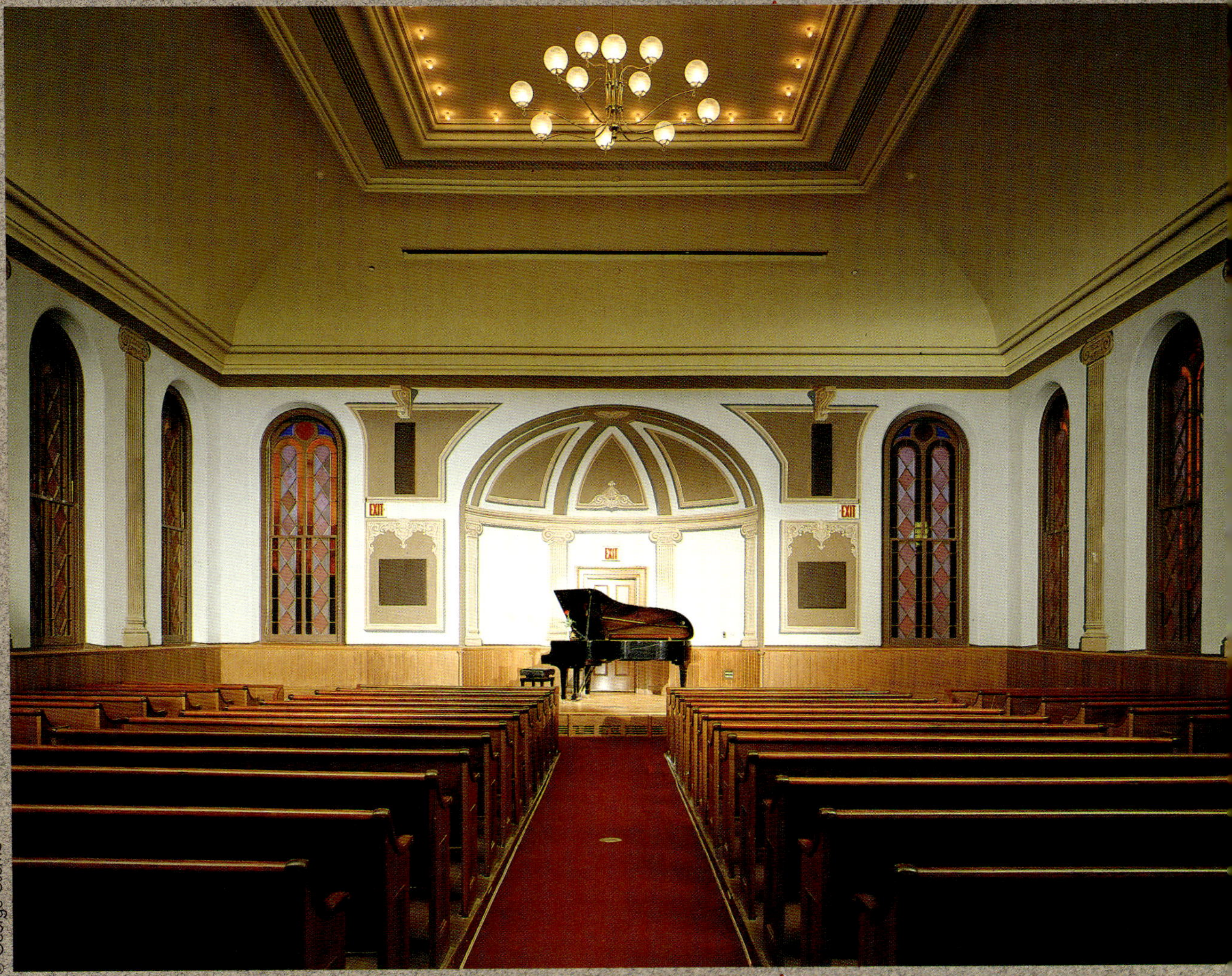

© George Cserna

defining needs, opportunities
and limitations;
responding to challenges
of budget and schedule;
creating spaces which function
with image and style.

© George Cserna Flowers: Gail Tracy

© Jay Rosenblatt

© Jay Rosenblatt

We offer our clients
experience, insight,
creativity, leadership.

We have a tradition of ongoing service to our clients

© Jay Rosenblatt

Together—managing change for the future.

© Robert I. Faulkner

Ryan Gibson Bauer Kornblath, PA
Architecture, Interior Architecture, Planning

One Arin Park
1715 State Highway 35
Middletown, NJ 07748
(201) 615-0100

Ninety West Street
New York, NY 10006
(212) 385-9090

Rivkin/Weisman

Rivkin/Weisman P.C.
Architects

141 Fifth Avenue
New York
New York 10010

212 473 6900

JUDGE US BY THE COMPANIES WE KEEP

American Stock Exchange
Automatic Data Processing
Bally Health and Tennis Corp.
Citibank N.A.
E.I. DuPont de Nemours
Equitable Life Assurance Society
Exxon Corporation
Mitsui International
The Morgan Guaranty Trust Co.
Morgan Stanley & Co., Inc.
New York Newsday
Ogilvy & Mather Direct
Republic National Bank
Saudi Petroleum International, Inc.
Shearson Lehman Hutton
Wang Laboratories
Warner Communications
Young & Rubicam Inc.

1114 First Avenue
New York, New York 10021
212/421-3500
FAX: 212/832-8346

SCR Design Organization, Inc.

Corporate Interior Designers
Facilities Consultants

SWANKE HAYDEN CONNELL ARCHITECTS

American Express—New York. Photo: Wolfgang Hoyt

Above: Television Studio, American Express—New York
Photo: Wolfgang Hoyt

Previous Page: Rivkin Radler Dunne & Bayh—Chicago
Photo: Nick Merrick/Hedrich Blessing

Fine Jacobson Schwartz Nash Block & England—Miami
Photo: Dan Forer

Swanke Hayden Connell Architects is a firm established in 1906 and which serves its clients in three major design areas: Interior Design, Architecture and Restoration. Versatility is the best way to describe the firm's approach to interior design for a distinguished list of Fortune 500 clients.

Assignments have varied from traditional designs to contemporary, from huge projects (over 2 million square feet) for American Express to small legal firms requiring 3,000 square feet. General tenancy areas get the same attention to detail as do executive spaces.

Swanke Hayden Connell Architects

400 Park Avenue
New York, New York 10022
(212) 826-1880

2 Illinois Center
233 North Michigan Avenue
Chicago, Illinois 60601
(312) 856-1090

1221 Brickell Avenue
Miami, Florida 33131
(305) 536-8600

12A Finsbury Square
London EC2A 1AS England
(011-441) 374-4371

The McPherson Building
901 Fifteenth Street, N.W.
Washington, D.C. 20005
(202) 393-0351

1988 AWARD FOR EXCELLENCE IN ARCHITECTURE
Northern Virginia Chapter AIA

1987 SMALL BUSINESS AWARD
Arlington Chamber of Commerce

PROUDLY PROVIDING ARCHITECTURAL SERVICES TO THE METROPOLITAN AREA SINCE 1958

SHERIDAN, BEHM, EUSTICE & ASSOCIATES, LTD.
A R C H I T E C T S A I A

Architects, Space Planners, Land Planners
Consultants, Commercial, Office, Multi Family
Educational and Religious Facilities

3440 Fairfax Drive • Arlington, Virginia 22201 • (703) 525-0270

ARCHITECTS AND DESIGNERS

SKYLINE

photography: O.C. Lee

principals

victor v. cacioppo r.a.
keith john milone r.a.

skyline architects pc
9 west 19th street,
new york, n.y. 10011
212•691•0801

SUMA INC.

THE MUTUAL EFFORT BETWEEN THE DESIGNER AND THE CLIENT, ALWAYS INCORPORATING EXPERIENCE AND CREATIVITY ▪ A UNIFIED SET OF IDEAS ▪ A COMMON VOCABULARY OF FORMS, MATERIALS AND COLOR ▪

INTERIOR DESIGN
ARCHITECTURE
PRODUCT DESIGN

236 WEST 27th STREET
NEW YORK, N.Y. 10001
TEL. 212-807-9590

CRAIG TOFTEY
45 MIDDLE STREET GLOUCESTER MASSACHUSETTS 01930-5736
PHONE 508-283-4494 MODEM 508-283-7514 FAX 508-281-3837

DIANNE B. BOUTIQUE New York, New York

X-O RESTAURANT New Jersey

FIRST EDITION VIDEO STUDIO New York

X-O RESTAURANT Garwood, New Jersey

Adaptive Rehabilitation, Banks, Furniture Designs, Hotels, Institutional and Educational: Dormitories, Libraries, Master Planning; Health Care/Science

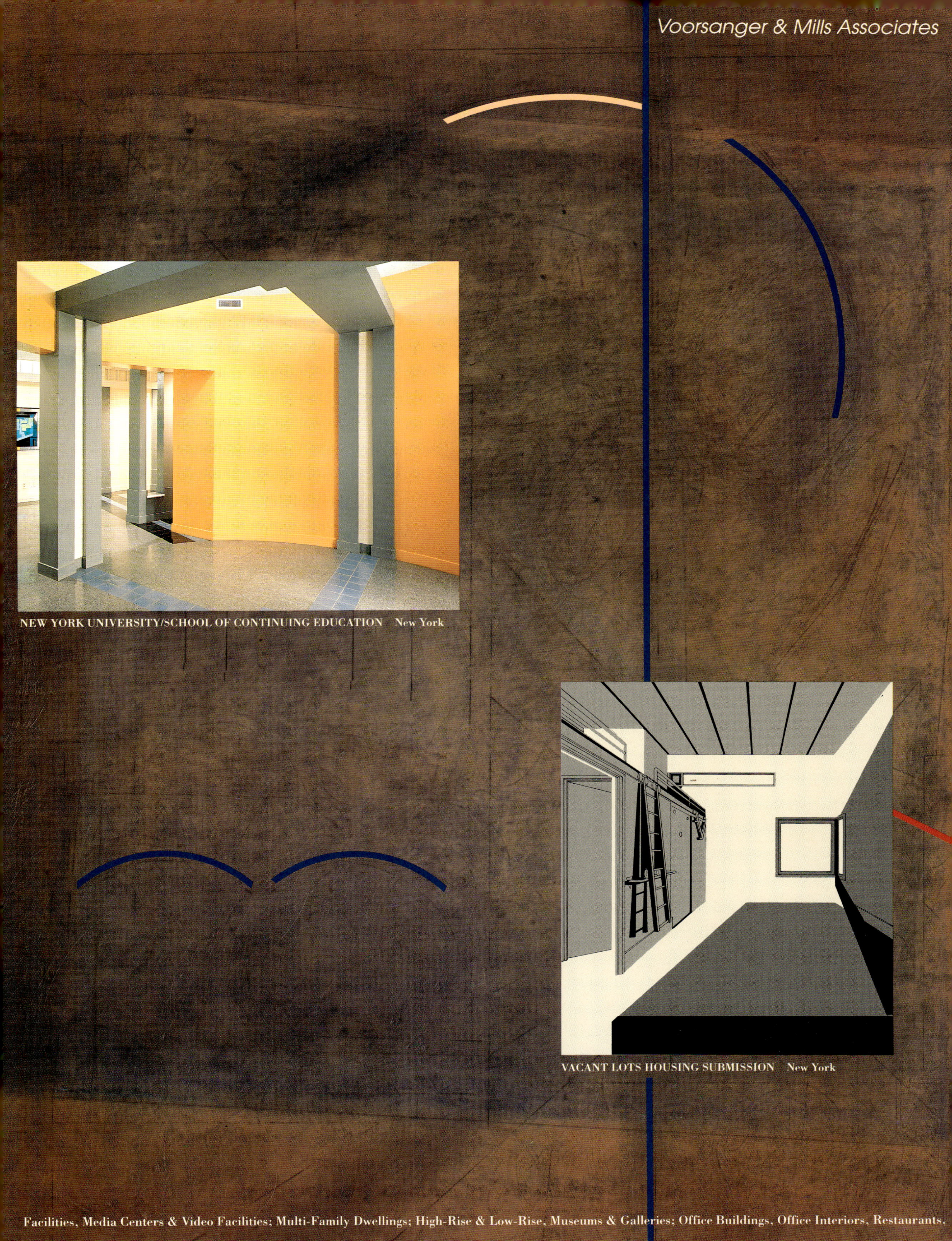

NEW YORK UNIVERSITY/SCHOOL OF CONTINUING EDUCATION New York

VACANT LOTS HOUSING SUBMISSION New York

Facilities, Media Centers & Video Facilities; Multi-Family Dwellings; High-Rise & Low-Rise, Museums & Galleries; Office Buildings, Office Interiors, Restaurants,

Voorsanger & Mills Associates
HOSTOS COMMUNITY COLLEGE Bronx, New York
Printed in Japan
Retail: Shops, Boutiques & Shopping Centers, Single-Family Dwellings
Voorsanger & Mills Associates
246 West Thirty-Eighth Street, New York, New York 10018, 212 302-6464

Walz Design Inc

Walz Design Inc
For More Details on Walz Design Contact Us at 141 Fifth Ave New York NY 10011 (212) 477 2211

YAB
SHELBERG

Founded in 1980 by George Yabu and Glenn Pushelberg, Yabu Pushelberg is a leader in the development of unique interior design. The projects include retail store design, corporate interiors, adaptive re-use, and large-scale mixed-use developments. They work with each client to determine their individual requirements; creating a space with a sense of identity. Exceptional detailing and consistently high quality of workmanship give emphasis to the strength of the design. Involvement is total, from the initial concept through to construction coordination. Their commitment is to fulfil the needs of the client, the space, and the market. The final product is an effective, dynamic, unified space: a creative, intelligent solution to the clients' needs.

L E S C O U R S M O N T R O Y A L

The central design problem is daring enough — a grand hotel as shopping environment. This 80 year old international landmark, in downtown Montreal, was converted into 300,000 square feet of upscale retail environment. Four levels of shops and services with sweeping staircases, curving balconies and light-filled halls, combine with the best of the Beaux Arts design legacy to create a unique urban shopping environment. The design process required that all current attitudes of the shopping mall be abandoned.

The most significant details and architectural elements of the original hotel were kept intact. In what was once the original hotel lobby, a newly designed grand staircase ceremoniously graces centre stage where it meets the refurbished crystal chandelier floating high above.

Beginning from traditional principles of moving people throughout the building's interior, graceful arcades, balconies, bridges and stairs were sensitively integrated. Lookouts such as a strategically positioned stair-landing allow arresting and often unusual perspectives of the multi-leveled and interconnected series of "courts".

Proportion has been carefully studied to achieve the necessary visual harmony when retro-fitting the base building for its newly acquired purpose. Ornamentation has been expressed without posturing. What is new has been sensitively interwoven into the original building fabric. Materials have been carefully chosen for their durability as much as for their character. Scale, material and surface treatment were carefully considered. Brushed steel and wrought iron echo the past but do not imitate it.

A timeless quality is sustained that allows the grand building to position itself once again as a gathering place for now and the future.

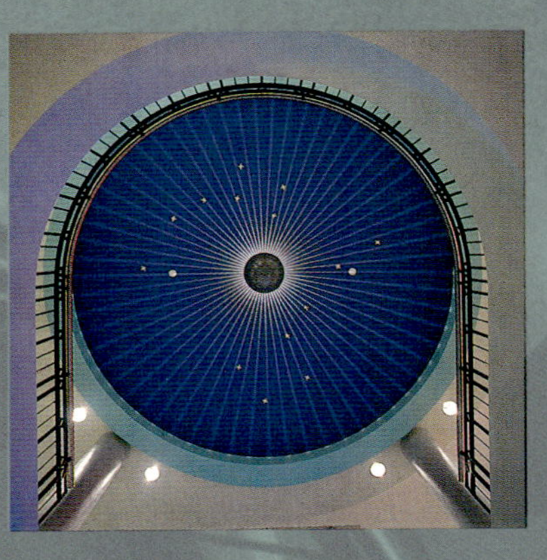

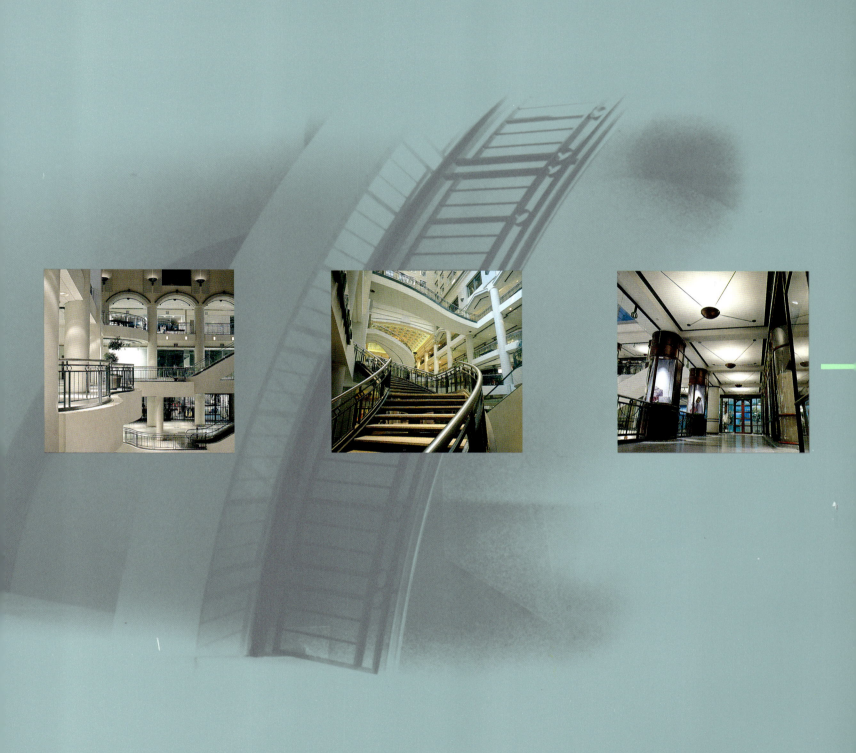

L E O N E

LEONE
LEONE
LEONE

Converting 14,000 square feet of Belle Époque Post Office into a European-type men's and women's fashion department store was a difficult challenge. Fortunately, this historically designated structure had 'good bones' for a conceptional framework.

The historical spine of the building, with an entrance to the street at one end and an enclosed shopping complex at the other, contained subtle mosaic tile floor patterns, historical wainscotting, original wall and ceiling mounted light fixtures and stained glass transom windows. The new tenant was presenting a collection of high-end fashion within seven distinct selling areas, each unique, dynamic and specific, while creating a unified visual attitude. It was important that a contemporary fashion view work in harmony with the historical references of the building.

Each in-store 'shop' is accessible from "La Strada", the spine of the complex, and main traffic path. Integrated into this historical storyboard are new custom designed fixtures housing the cosmetics, perfumes, gifts, and confections departments. Sprinkled in between, are display podiums, announcing the entranceway to a new department. All new fixtures were intentionally designed on legs so that the existing mosaic tile floor pattern would be observed. The fixturing, an ivory coloured painted wood with charcoal stain rubbed into the grain was scaled to integrate and harmonize with the existing historical mouldings.

The design solutions for each department are meant to reinforce the sophistication and elegance of the merchandise on display. The interiors project a sense of humour, art, surprise and intrigue, with a constant sense of discovery as one progresses through the various departments.

S T I L L I F E

'Stilife', a 7500 square foot basement night club in Toronto's garment district has all the necessary elements for entertaining Ginza sophisticates or world-weary Berliners.

As a reflection of its location and potential clientele, international art and fashion play an inspirational role in the interiors. Images from European art movements confront tribal shields, hieroglyphics, raw materials and high technology. The drink rails personify this radical mix. Wrought iron surrealist tree forms support traditional mosaic tops patterned with aboriginal hieroglyphics while the light pattern nearby emits a machine-like precision. This rich palette could equally be found on the fashion runways of Milan or Tokyo.

As the name implies, low street level exterior windows have been turned over to window displays in the European still life tradition. This sampling of the 'moods' offered inside is also similar to the highly crafted models of sushi many Japanese restaurants use to proclaim their menu.

While not a Japanese karaoke bar in practice, the operation is definitely one of 'adult play'. Image-laden seating groups have been created in the quiet room. The 3-D mural and high vinyl pill sofa bring a sixties pop feeling to one part of the room. Other metaphors include a surrealist lip sofa/face elevation or a cave-like rock pit adjacent. Patrons are encouraged to choose their 'stilife' setting for the evening.

The main space is presented through a holding area defined by a series of portals in a diagonal wall. Each portal frames the stilife of the moment.

We find an allusion to the traditional Japanese water theme. In the holding area, a techno-pop water sculpture utilizes a combination of air pressure and edge lighting to create luminescent air bubbles which rise through a 2" thick acrylic abstract pachinko game.

This polyglot of images and materials; the familiar and the provocative; the ascetic and the deluxe; the real and the imagined; create an interior dedicated to the night.

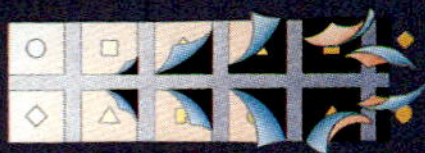

Yabu Pushelberg
359 King St. E., Toronto, Ont. M5A 1L1
(416) 362-1414 Fax (416) 362-8909

Z B I N C

227 WEST 17TH STREET

NEW YORK, NY 10011

212 • 242 • 1991

D E S I G N

ITT PRODUCT CENTER • PHOTOGRAPHY: MARK ROSS

CORPORATE INTERIORS • SPACE PLANNING • RETAIL DESIGN

INTERIOR
DESIGN
RETAIL

Beyer Blinder Belle

Interiors

Barneys New York

The Limited Express

South Street Seaport Pub

Aquascutum, Chicago

The Limited, NY

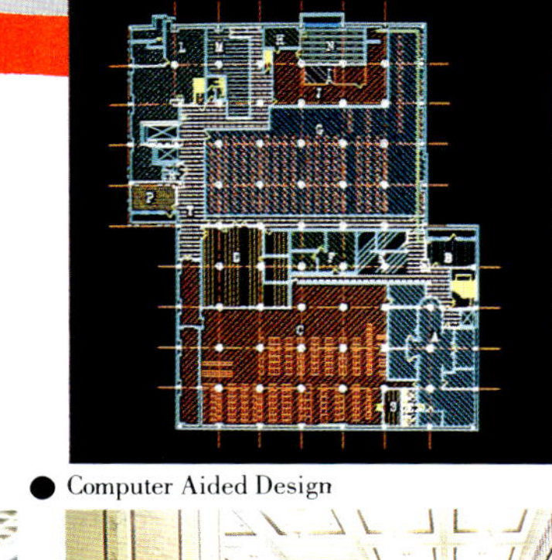

Computer Aided Design

CBS, New York

Gair #7, Brooklyn

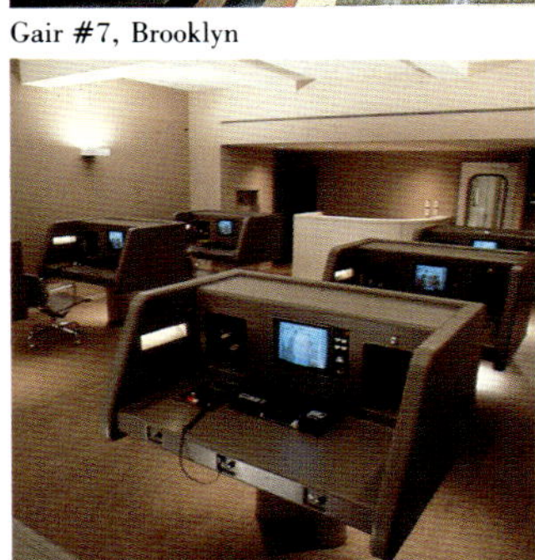

Museum of Broadcasting

CBS, New York

Estee Lauder

Facilities Programming
Building Analysis
Leasing Support
Design
Construction Documents
Cost Control
Furniture, Accessories & Graphics
Art Selection

Beyer Blinder Belle

Interiors

Historic and Landmark Interiors Museums and Public Buildings Corporate Offices Retail Stores and Restaurants Libraries

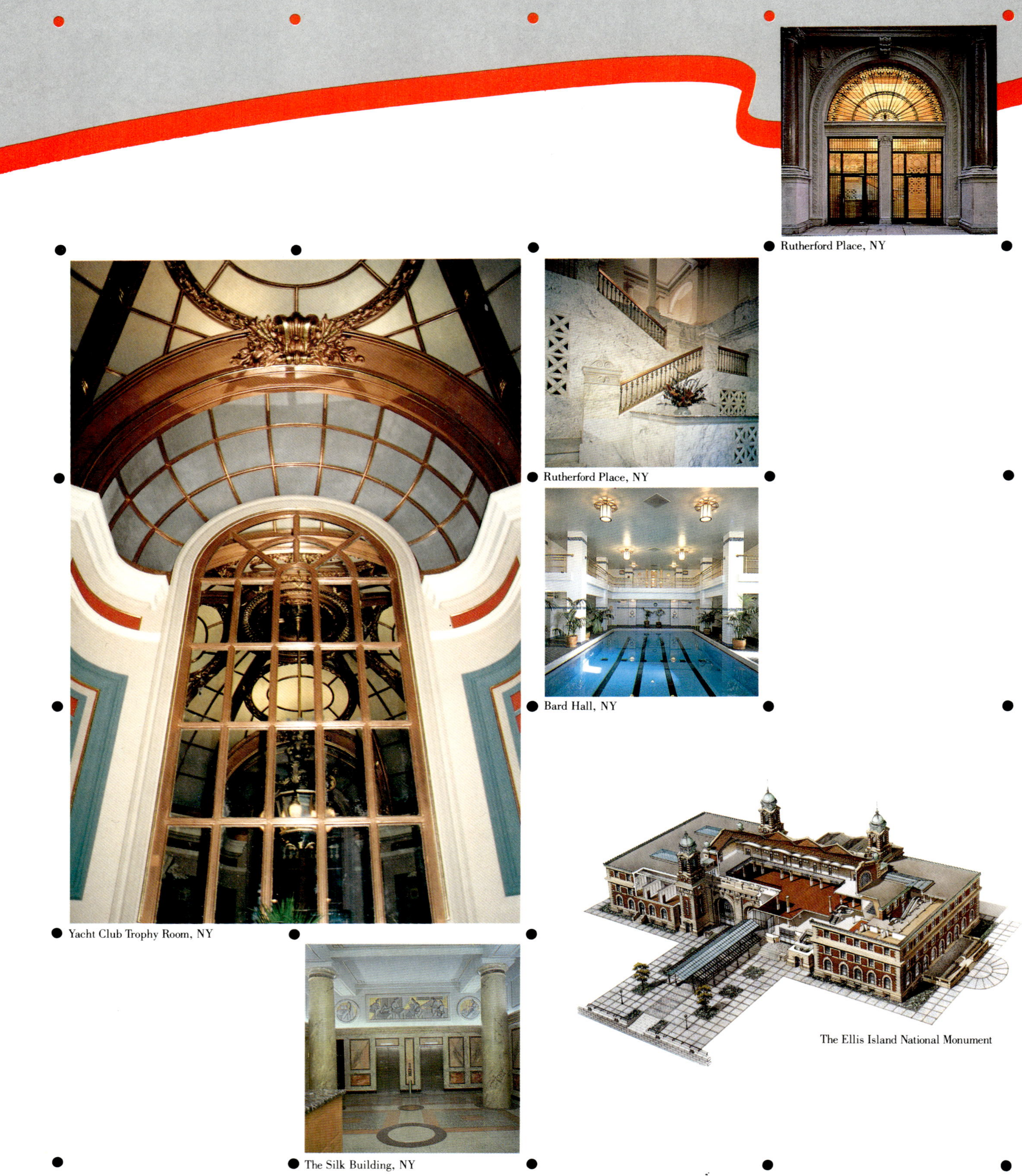

Rutherford Place, NY

Yacht Club Trophy Room, NY

Rutherford Place, NY

Bard Hall, NY

The Silk Building, NY

The Ellis Island National Monument

Beyer Blinder Belle 41 East 11 Street New York, New York 10003 212 777 7800 FAX 212 475-7424

ANDREW S. BLACKMAN A.I.A. ARCHITECT

Concepts International Showroom, New York City

International China Showroom, New York City

Alexander Julian Showroom, New York City

British Caledonian Airlines Ticket Office, New York City

Denby Showroom, New York City

Champ Hats Showroom, New York City

Andrew S. Blackman A.I.A. • Architect • 121 East 36th Street • New York City 10016 • (212) MUrray Hill 3-4884

JANOVIC PLAZA

JAMES D'AURIA ASSOCIATES ARCHITECTS

12 W. 27 ST. NEW YORK, NY 10001 212-725-5660 FAX: 212-725-5698

PHOTO: NATHANIEL LIEBERMAN

GUESS ?, INC.

MEMBERS ONLY

ADRIENNE VITTADINI

STEILMANN BOUTIQUE

JAMES D'AURIA ASSOCIATES
ARCHITECTS

12 W. 27 ST. NEW YORK, NY 10001 212-725-5660 FAX: 212-725-5698

PHOTOS: NORMAN McGRATH PAUL WARCHOL AMBROSE CUCINOTTA

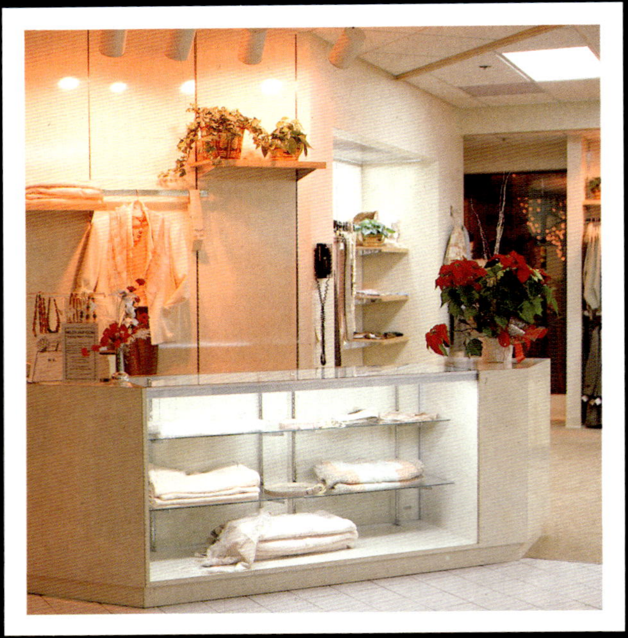

1

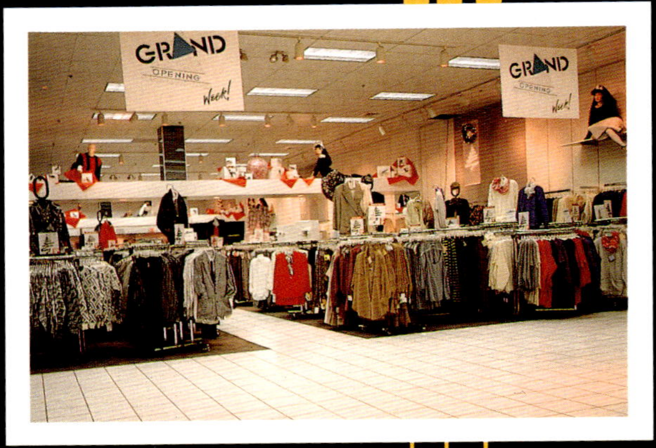

2

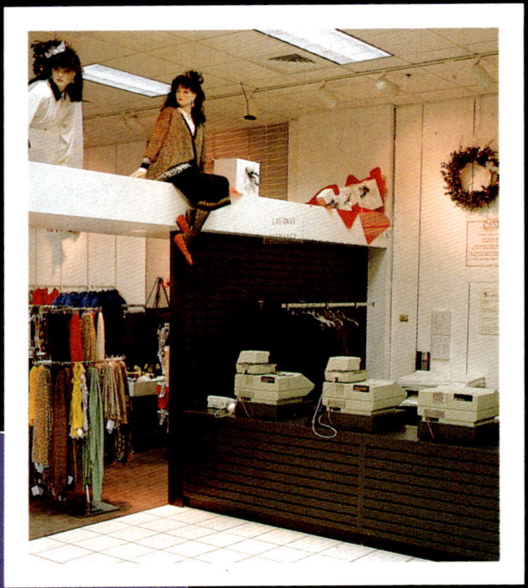

3

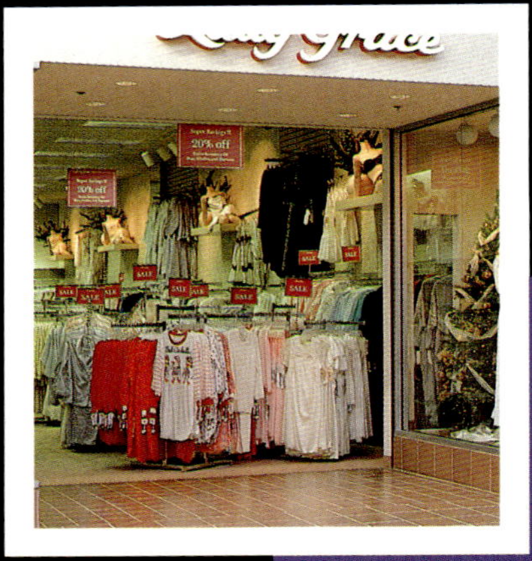

4

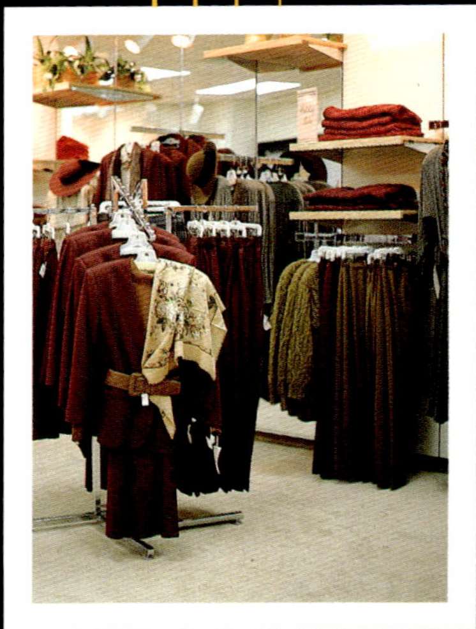

5

34 Commerce Way
Woburn, Mass. 01801
(617) 935-5200

De Stefano Studios, Inc., Total Store Planning Services for the New England area. We'll take your ideas from concept through construction to completion. We supply everything for the retailer: mannequins and forms, display props, a complete line of store fixtures and custom woodworking.

1. Helen Olevson
   Baystate West Mall
   Springfield, MA.
2. Tello's
   Greendale Mall
   Worcester, MA.
3. Tello's
   Greendale Mall
   Worcester, MA.
4. Lady Grace
   Greendale Mall
   Worcester, MA.
5. Helen Olevson
   Baystate West Mall
   Springfield, MA.

CHARLES DAMGA
DESIGN

DESIGN

CORPORATE
RESIDENTIAL
RETAIL
MEDIA EVENT
MODEL APARTMENT
RESTAURANT
SHOWROOM
FURNITURE

© 1989 Concept Publications Inc. Printed in Japan.

812 BROADWAY NYC 10003 533 8555

Marc Alpert, Italian Collection, New York

Freego USA, New York

D . P . I . D . INC

Knowing the wholesale marketplace and their vendors, and understanding the consumer and their changing ways; how they live, play, work and shop, forms the foundation of D.P.I.D. Inc.'s design philosophy in approaching designs for business which are more responsive to environments.

We bring about solutions which achieve the client's goals.

Marc Alpert Showroom, New York

Genesis, Carson Pirie Scott, Chicago

Mexx, Bloomingdale's, New York

DOMINICK PARISI INTERIOR DESIGN
#1 UNION SQUARE WEST SUITE 609 • NEW YORK, NY 10003

Bloomingdale's, White Plains, New York

Bloomie's Express, John F. Kennedy International Airport, New York, New York

Chanel, Braintree, Massachusetts

Dayton Hudson Department Store Company, Lancome, Briarwood Mall, Ann Arbor, Michigan

Fitzpatrick Design Group

2109 Broadway, Suite 203, New York, New 10023 • (212) 580-5842

Bloomingdale's 6th Floor (Flagship store), New York, New York

Godiva Chocolatier, New York, New York

Bloomingdale's, White Plains, New York

Dayton Hudson Department Store Company, Briarwood Mall, Ann Arbor, Michigan

Fitzpatrick Design Group

2109 Broadway, Suite 203, New York, New 10023 • (212) 580-5842

BLOOMINGDALE'S
Boulevard on Four
New York, N.Y.

PETER PAIGE

A full service architectural/interior design firm specializing in the conception and creation of retail environments.

HAMBRECHT TERRELL INTERNATIONAL
860 BROADWAY
NEW YORK, NEW YORK 10003
212 • 254 • 1229

Margaret
Helfand
Architects
32
East 38
Street
New York
10016
212
779 7260

Jacobs & Pratt Inc.

Consultants in Interior Design,
Retail Planning, Architectural Design,
Industrial Design & Graphic Design

In Detail

The soft-curved mahogany cabinetry surrounds a patterned Italian marble rotunda and sets the stage for luxurious linens and accessories for bed and bath. Complimenting wood with brass carts and gondolas are customized to provide presentation flexibility for the various merchandise collections. Low-voltage lighting over strategically located displays entice the customer through the store.

Meridian

Honed verdi antique marble and undulating walls of natural finished ash provide the setting for this contemporary sportswear shop. Pools of light, created by illuminated ceiling treatments over the display points, define flexible swing shops as well as reinforce traffic flow.

J&P

270 Lafayette Street
New York, NY 10012
212, 226, 3994

chic
EXIT

chic

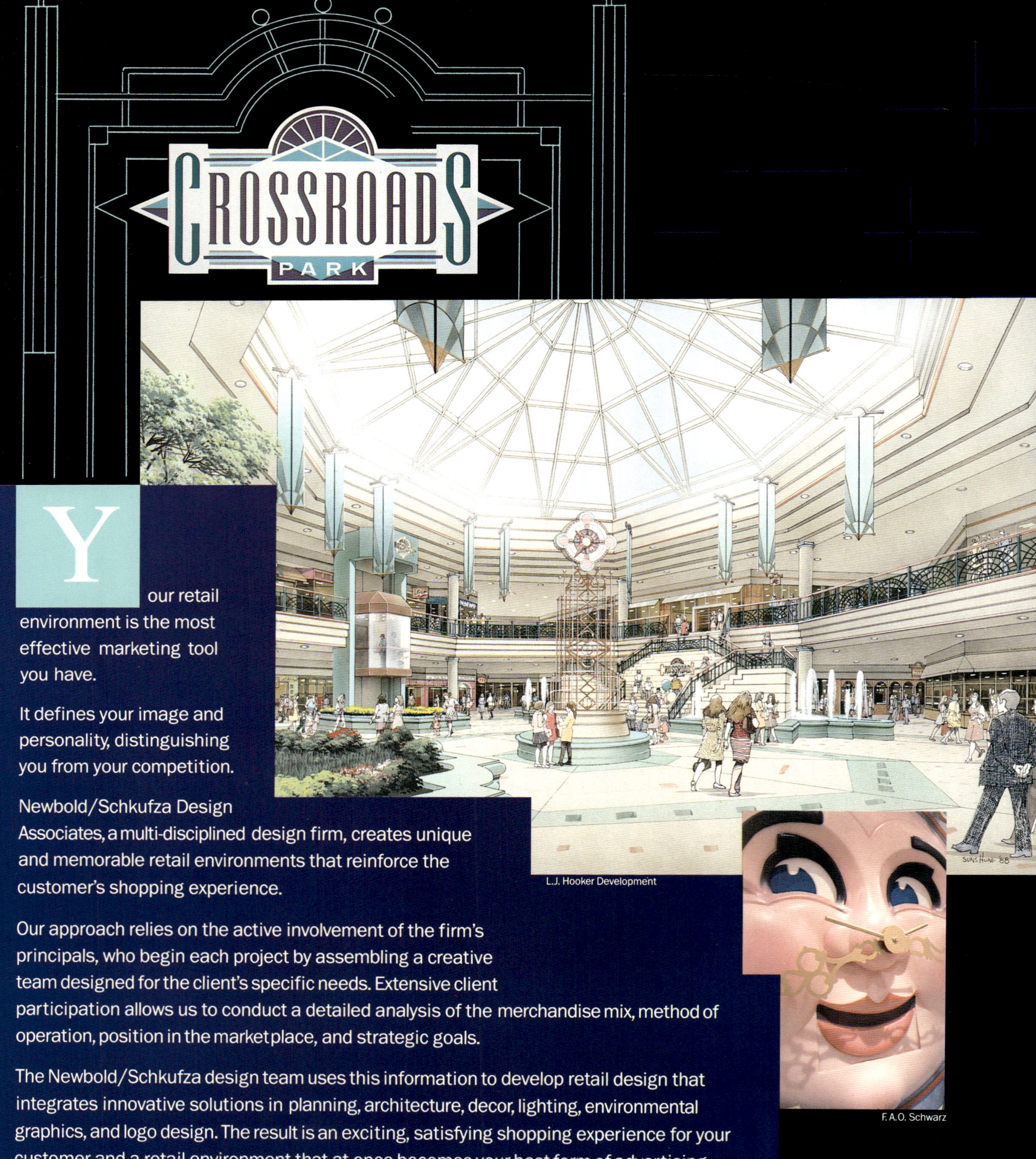

CROSSROADS
PARK
Your retail environment is the most effective marketing tool you have.
It defines your image and personality, distinguishing you from your competition.
Newbold/Schkufza Design Associates, a multi-disciplined design firm, creates unique and memorable retail environments that reinforce the customer's shopping experience.
Our approach relies on the active involvement of the firm's principals, who begin each project by assembling a creative team designed for the client's specific needs. Extensive client participation allows us to conduct a detailed analysis of the merchandise mix, method of operation, position in the marketplace, and strategic goals.
The Newbold/Schkufza design team uses this information to develop retail design that integrates innovative solutions in planning, architecture, decor, lighting, environmental graphics, and logo design. The result is an exciting, satisfying shopping experience for your customer and a retail environment that at once becomes your best form of advertising, building on your reputation in the marketplace.

L.J. Hooker Development

F.A.O. Schwarz

Newbold **Schkufza**

DESIGN ASSOCIATES

Miami International Airport

full circle

F.A.O. Schwarz

TSR
OVAL ROOM
TUCCI SEGRETE AND ROSEN CONSULTANTS

T.S.R. is an innovative organization specializing in design and concept development. Our staff, a team of carefully selected creative designers, planners, project coordinators, technicians and architects are in position to propel retailers into the next century. T.S.R. is committed to its clients' needs and creates environments that are unique, well merchandised, on schedule and on budget.

Awards

1988 First Place—Chain Store Executive Store of the Year

1988 First Prize—ISP/NRMA International Store Interior Design Competition

1987 First Place—Chain Store Executive Store of the Year

1987 Design Solution Award of Excellence

1984 N.A.D.I.

1984 National Mall Monitor Award

Clients

ALLIED
BELK
BEST CO.
BORSHEIMS
B. DALTON
COOKWORLD
DAYTON HUDSON DEPARTMENT STORE CO.
EATON CO.
FRANCESCA GIRARD
FINANCIAL FEDERAL
FORTUNOFF
GONZALEZ PADIN CO.
HAHNE & CO.
JOSEPH HORNE CO. INC.
LAZARUS
MARSHALL FIELD
MAY DEPARTMENT STORES CO.
MACKAYS
MILLERS OUTPOST
R.G. BRANDENS
SAKS FIFTH AVENUE
SAIL U.S.A.
LINDSAY & CURR CO.
STATE SAVINGS & LOAN
THALHIMERS

TSR
TUCCI, SEGRETE & ROSEN
CONSULTANTS, INC
440 NINTH AVENUE
NEW YORK, NY. 10001
212 • 629 • 3900

WalkerGroup/CNI Graphic Design

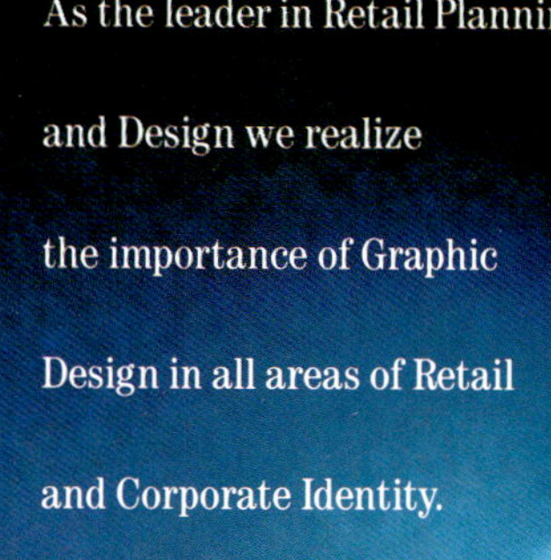

As the leader in Retail Planning and Design we realize the importance of Graphic Design in all areas of Retail and Corporate Identity.

FAO Schwarz, New York, NY

Did you know that Graphic Design can...

Please contact
Marketing Department

WalkerGroup/CNI
320 West 13th Street
New York
New York 10014
Telephone (212) 206 0444

The Carnival,
Evansville, IN

. . . Reflect the exciting and evolving fashion environment

from Public and Retail spaces to Package Design . . .

Pompano Square Mall, Pompano Beach, FL

Singles, Dallas, TX

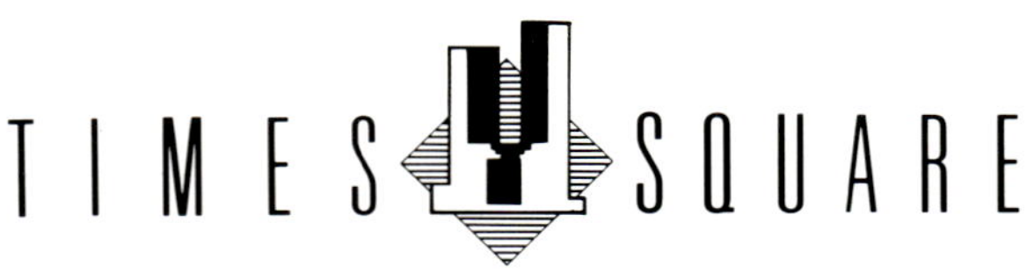

. . . Create unique identities reflecting the quality and position

of the client and the customer he serves . . .

. . . Confirm not only the Visual Identity and Presence of

the total Retail Environment . . .

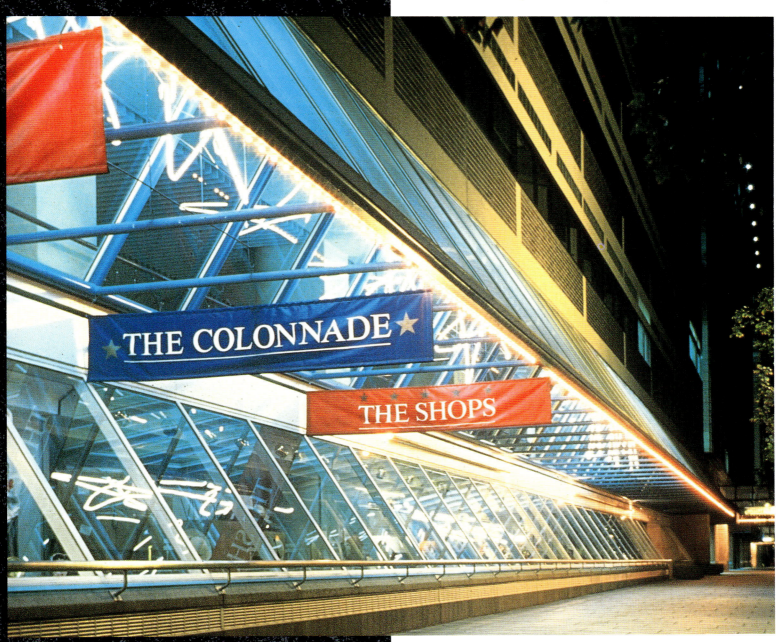

The Shops At National Place, Washington, DC

. . . But also reflect the Spirit

of the surrounding community . . .

. . . Achieve the successful translation of a Corporate Identity

from Packaging to Collateral Material . . .

Almay, New York, NY

Laderach,
Godiva Chocolatiers,
New York, NY

Maxx, Amstore Systems,
Chicago, IL

. . . Translate a Corporate or Retail Identity into

a consumer friendly environment

and a customer accessible package!

INTERIOR
DESIGN
HEALTH CARE

"Medicinal Arts...

Rarely do the medical office and the art gallery inspire comparison; this facility, however, narrows the gap between their extremes..."

The design invites visitors from the moment they step off the elevator...

Simple, sleek and refined, this office delights the aesthetic eye..."

PROFESSIONAL OFFICE DESIGN
May/June 1988

Kenneth Blaustein + Associates Design

41 Union Square West, Suite 1428
New York, NY 10003
(212) 206-7506

SPECIALISTS IN

HEALTH

CARE

ARCHITECTURE

&

INTERIOR

DESIGN

Taylor Clark Architects, Inc. TCA
149 Fifth Avenue New York, NY 10010-6801 212-460-8840

ROGERS, BURGUN, SHAHINE & DESCHLER, INC. ARCHITECTS

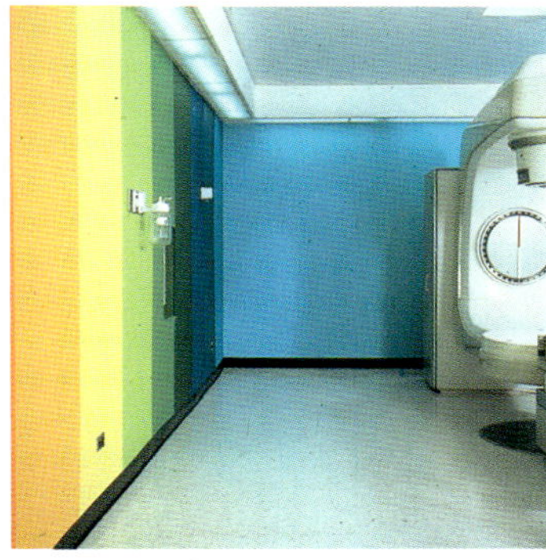

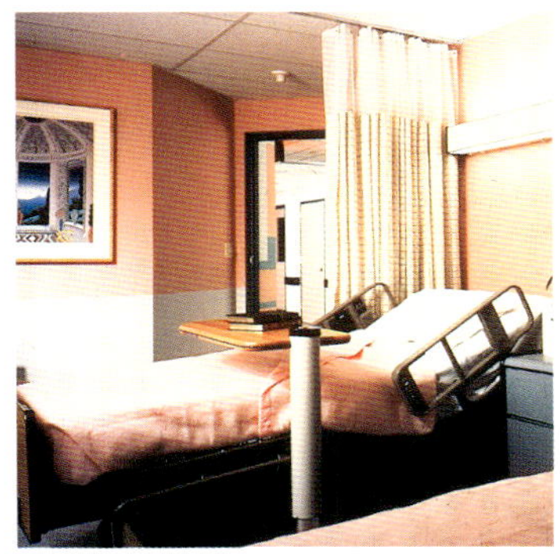

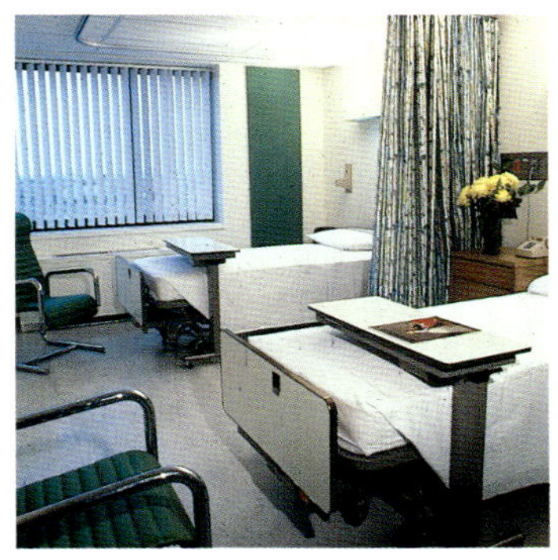

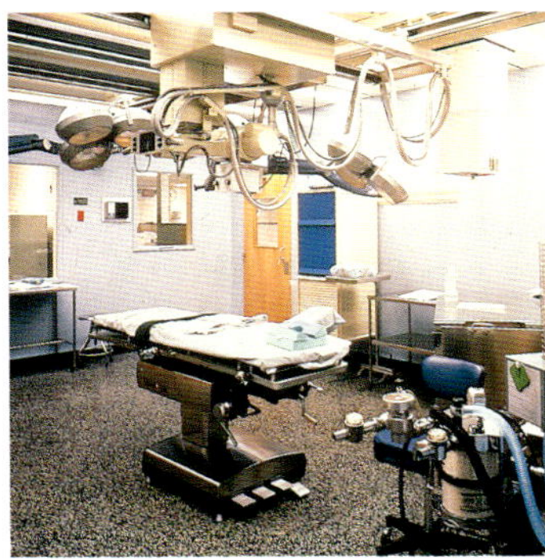

RBSD

Rogers, Burgun, Shahine and Deschler, Inc. Architects

215 Park Avenue South
New York, NY 10003
212-614-0788

Telex 640-401 RBSD
FAX 212-529-8710

Rogers, Burgun, Shahine & Deschler, Inc. is an architectural firm noted for the design and planning of healthcare projects. Founded in 1908 and in continuous practice since then, RBSD has designed and completed over 400 institutional facilities at an unescalated value of more than 3 1/2 billion dollars in construction cost.

INTERIOR
DESIGN
HOSPITALITY

ALMASIAN ASSOCIATES INC.

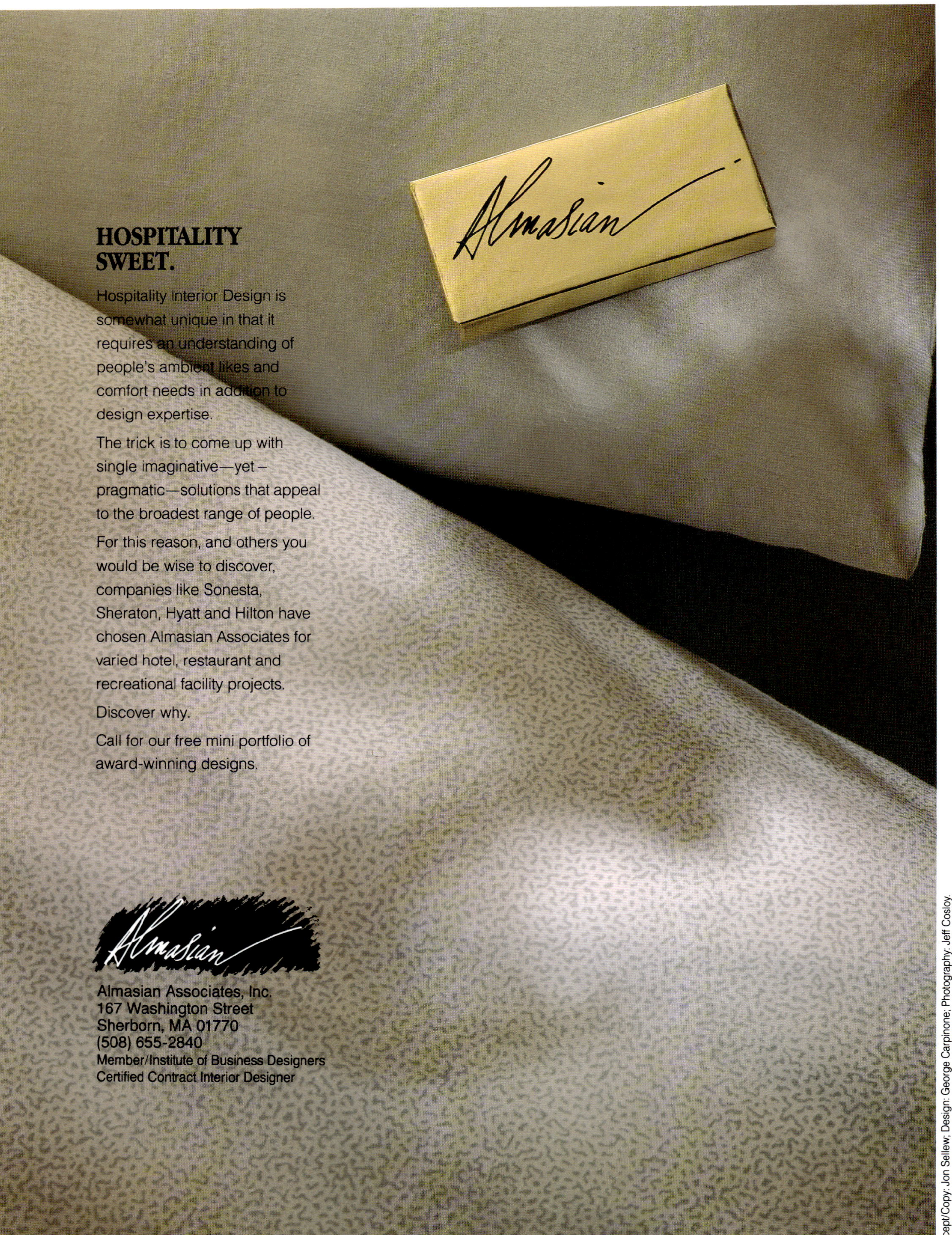
Almasian
HOSPITALITY SWEET.
Hospitality Interior Design is somewhat unique in that it requires an understanding of people's ambient likes and comfort needs in addition to design expertise.
The trick is to come up with single imaginative—yet—pragmatic—solutions that appeal to the broadest range of people.
For this reason, and others you would be wise to discover, companies like Sonesta, Sheraton, Hyatt and Hilton have chosen Almasian Associates for varied hotel, restaurant and recreational facility projects.
Discover why.
Call for our free mini portfolio of award-winning designs.
Almasian
Almasian Associates, Inc.
167 Washington Street
Sherborn, MA 01770
(508) 655-2840
Member/Institute of Business Designers
Certified Contract Interior Designer

SAMUEL BOTERO ASSOCIATES, INC.

Photographs: Phillip Ennis

150 East 58 Street, 23 Floor, New York, N.Y. 10155/212•935•5155

SAMUEL BOTERO ASSOCIATES, INC.
150 East 58 Street, 23 Floor, New York, N.Y. 10155/212•935•5155

photos by Jim Daddio

Sultan Blaustein Associates
Design Group

41 Union Square West, Suite 307
New York, NY 10003
(212) 206-7506
(212) 807-1344

1-10

mley/Jacobsen

Architecture & Design

242 W
New Y
212 62

2
1
2
▼
3
5
3
▼
8
8
6
0

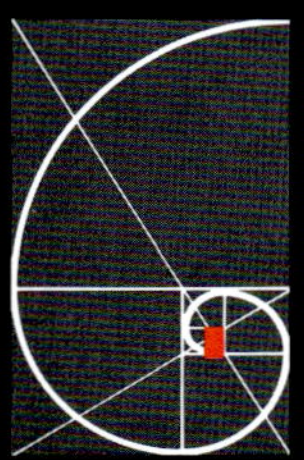

611 Broadway

Suite 724

New York, NY 10012

D O N G H I A

315 East 62 Street New York, New York 10021 212 486 1100

DONGHIA ASSOCIATES

Known for both residential and contract design, Donghia Associates' projects include the S.S. Norway, Trump Tower and other residential buildings; offices, showrooms, corporate and model apartments; Doral, Omni, and InterContinental hotel chains.

D O N G H I A

315 East 62 Street New York, New York 10021 212 486 1100

HAVERSON/ROCKWELL ARCHITECTS, P.C.

Haverson/Rockwell Architects, P.C., an award-winning, innovative design firm, provides a full spectrum of services—master planning, architectural design, interior and lighting design, graphics, and economic feasibility studies—to a growing list of international corporations, development companies, and individuals. Our project record includes a wide variety of building types and uses, including restaurants, commercial space, residences, office areas, and health and fitness centers. Every project, regardless of size or budget, receives the personal attention of the principals of the firm. The emphasis is on creating a distinctive, meaningful environment that fits the client's needs.

View from the uppermost dining tier. "Twenty:Twenty" restaurant, New York, NY.

Bar detail, "Il Bianco" restaurant, New York, NY.

Al Fresco dining on the terrace at "Il Bianco" restaurant, New York, NY.

The central "fish market" display area, viewed from the entry. "Big Splash" restaurant, North Miami Beach, Florida.

Gated entry to the platform dining area at "The Tribeca Cafe," New York, NY.

The center aisle lighting technique dramatically expands the interior space at "Sushi-Zen" restaurant in New York City.

"The Ocean Reef Grille" located at the South Street Seaport in New York City combines an uplit ceiling with various types of boats from the Seaport collection.

NOBUTAKA ASHIHARA ASSOCIATES
37 MURRAY STREET NEW YORK, NEW YORK 10007
(212) 233-1783

ELEGANT DINING;
COMFORTABLE SPACING,
OLD WORLD MATERIALS AND
ATTENTION TO DETAILS
WITH UNCOMPROMISED
CRAFTSMANSHIP.
ABOVE: BAR, QV
NEW YORK, NY
RIGHT: DINING ROOM, QV
NEW YORK, NY

FOOD FOR THOUGHT;
AWARD WINNING RESTAURANT
DESIGN, INTERIOR DESIGN,
MENU CONSULTATION

TASTE DESIGN

AND GRAPHIC DESIGN.
CHARLES MORRIS MOUNT, INC.
MOUNT AND COMPANY

GREAT DESIGN SELLS; MERCHANDISING AND MARKETING THE DESIGN SOLUTION, IMAGE DEVELOPMENT AND INTEGRATION OF OVERALL DESIGN CONCEPT.

TOP: PIZZERIA UNO
SECAUCUS, NJ
ABOVE LEFT: MARKET,
AMERICAN CAFE
TYSON'S CORNER, VA
ABOVE RIGHT: BAR,
AMERICAN CAFE
TYSON'S CORNER, VA

INTIMATE SPACES; REFLECTIONS OF PERSONAL STYLE, SOFT LIGHTING AND WARM FINISHES.

ABOVE: RESIDENCE
NEW YORK, NY
RIGHT: CHEZ MA TANTE
NEW YORK, NY

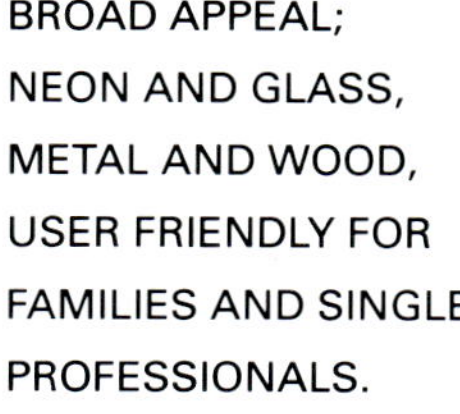

BROAD APPEAL;
NEON AND GLASS,
METAL AND WOOD,
USER FRIENDLY FOR
FAMILIES AND SINGLE
PROFESSIONALS.
ABOVE LEFT: AMERICAN CAFE
WASHINGTON, DC
ABOVE RIGHT: CAFE BAR,
AMERICAN CAFE
WASHINGTON, DC
RIGHT: WEST END CAFE
CARLE PLACE, NY

CORPORATE DESIGN;
INTERIOR ARCHITECTURE,
LIGHTING, MATERIALS, FINISHES
AND FURNITURE SELECTION.
ABOVE: DESIGN TEX SHOWROOM
HOUSTON, TX
RIGHT: DESIGN TEX SHOWROOM
WASHINGTON, DC

INNOVATIVE IDEAS;
FAST FOOD WITH FLAIR,
FAMILY DINING WITH FINESSE,
UNIQUE COMBINATION OF
MATERIALS AND PRAGMATIC
RESEARCH WITH AN INNATE
SENSE OF DESIGN.

TOP LEFT: BAR, MR. STEAK
WINSTON-SALEM, NC
TOP RIGHT: McDONALDS
ROCKEFELLER CENTER
NEW YORK, NY
ABOVE: GREENHOUSE ROOM,
MR. STEAK
WINSTON-SALEM, NC

CHARLES MORRIS MOUNT, INC.
RESIDENTIAL DESIGN
MOUNT AND COMPANY
RESTAURANT DESIGN
INTERIOR ARCHITECTURE
MENU CONSULTATION
GRAPHIC DESIGN
104 WEST 27 STREET
NEW YORK, NY 10001
212-807-0800
FAX: 212 727-2383

PHOTO CREDITS: NORMAN McGRATH, SCOTT FRANCES, H. DURSTON SAYLOR, ELLIOT KAUFMAN, TOM YEE, BENT RAY, ROBERT MILLER

NORDSTROM

NEW YORK, NEW YORK

212 - 675 - 6772

The Hair Cutting Place
Toronto

Rainbows
Miami

Le Connaisseur
Toronto

Mark III Productions
Miami

Rafaell Cabrera International

914 Yonge Street
Suite 1701
Toronto, Ontario
M4W 3C8
(416) 964-6947
(416) 964-8678

246 West End Avenue
Suite 2B
New York, New York
10023
(212) 787-3851

Rafaell Cabrera
Dennis Abbé

Extra! Extra!
New York

Lox Around The Clock, New York
Photo © 1989 Mark Roskam

Lox Around The Clock, New York
Photo © 1989 Donna Day

Cafe Marimba, New York
Photos © 1989 Peter Paige

Coastal, New York
Photo © 1989 Masao Uerda

Coastal, New York
Photo © 1989 Karen Halverson

Batons, New York
Photos © Peter Paige

Java Bay
Tokyo
Photos © 1989 Hiruyuki Hirai

Java Jive
Tokyo
Photos © 1989 Hiruyuki Hirai

VALERIAN RYBAR & DAIGRE DESIGN CORP.

DESIGNERS OF SOME OF AMERICA'S MOST PRESTIGIOUS RESTAURANTS

Le Régence	Hotel Plaza Athénée	New York, NY
Polo Restaurant	Westbury Hotel	New York, NY
Cafe Pierre & Ballroom	Hotel Pierre	New York, NY
Doubles	Private Club	New York, NY
Capriccio Restaurant	Resorts International	Atlantic City, NJ
L'Orangerie Restaurant	(Pictured Above)	Los Angeles, CA

INTERIOR DESIGN MODEL SUITES

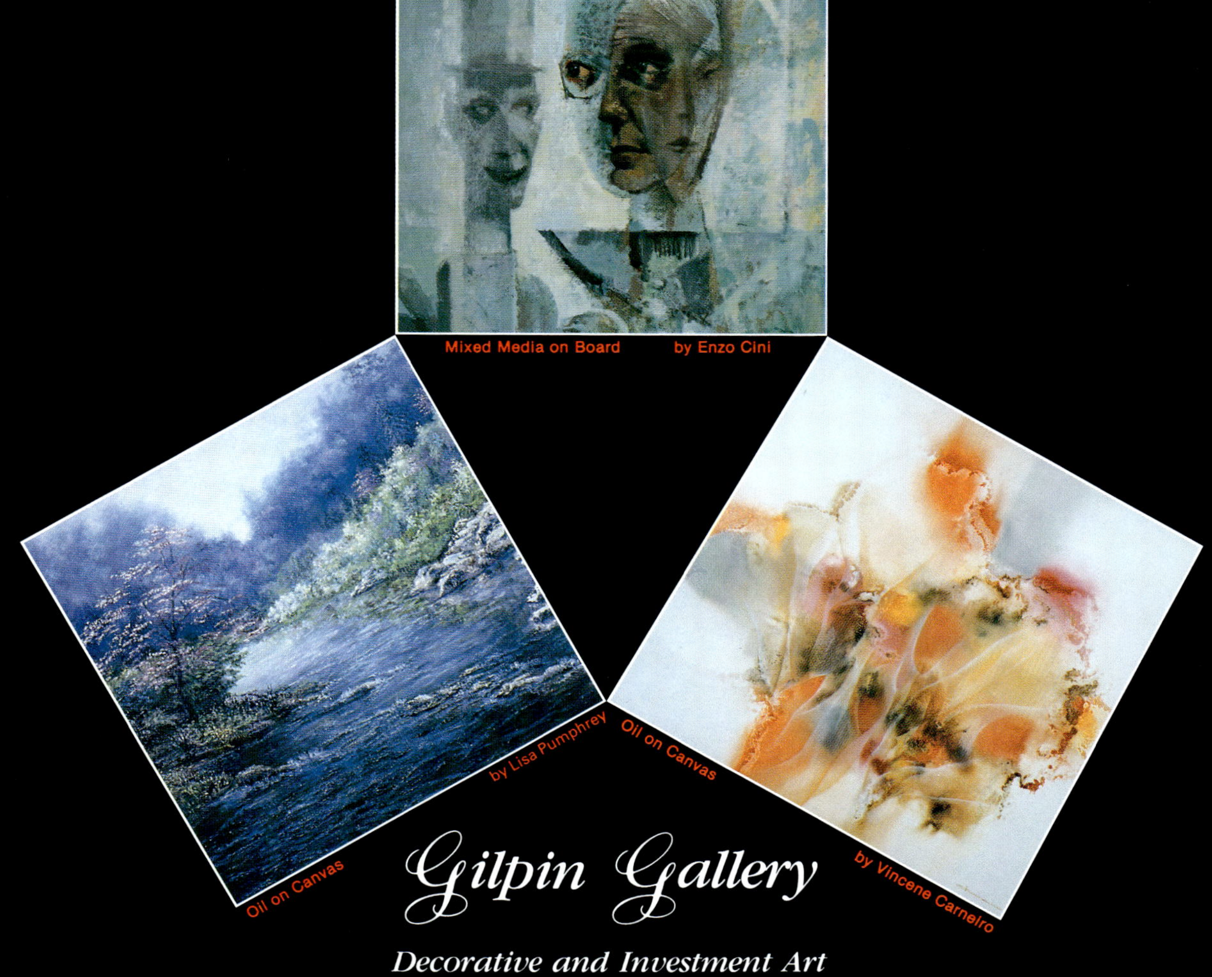

Mixed Media on Board by Enzo Cini
Oil on Canvas by Lisa Pumphrey
Oil on Canvas by Vincene Carneiro
Gilpin Gallery
Decorative and Investment Art

The Gilpin Gallery is fully committed to client service and will work with you through all phases of art selection. Whether you are looking for one perfect painting for that special spot in your home or a complete are theme for a corporate office, please allow us to assist you.

Our Services Include:

- Quality selections of original or reproduction art reflecting your budgetary requirements, decor and taste.
- Museum Framing as required.
- Proper Installation.
- Biographies of artists for your records.
- Research to locate your art requirements.
- Fine Sculpture.

Proprietors: Maryanne Kowalesky & Helen Nelson

One Prince Street • Olde Towne • Alexandria, VA 22314 • (703) 836-0110 or (703) 683-1736

GUENTER ROESLER ASSOCIATES INC.
286 CONGRESS STREET BOSTON MASSACHUSETTS 02210 617 426-4910

Alex Chapman Design Ltd.

depth understanding of both the

architecture of the building and the

lifestyle of the people who will live

there. But that's just the beginning.

Within a lobby, sales office or model

suite, many more elements come into

play: light, line, colour, texture

rhythm – and the harmony created

across Canada and the United States.

The company's distinctive work is

known for its strong lines, interplay of

textures and sophisticated colour

palette. At times the design is bold:

the firm is not timid in its use of over-

scale elements – nor with its sense of

humour. The work of Alex Chapman

the
condominiums
ESPLANADE

Strong interior design is an integral part of a successful condominium marketing plan. A team player, Alex Chapman Design works together with developers to build well-defined, accessible spaces. Then once the dynamic flow of space is established, the company's professionals begin to shape the final elements. It's the attention to detail and mature eclecticism of Chapman's award-winning design that ensures its longevity.

49 Spadina Ave., Suite 507, Toronto
Canada M5V 2J1, 416 597 1576

NORMA KING DESIGN INC.

BOSTON, NEW YORK, TORONTO, MIAMI

SADDLE BROOK, TORONTO

The elements are simple yet powerful: colour, form, texture, light, rhythm.

Successful interior design is a harmonizing of all these motifs.

At Norma King Design, we create that delicate balance.

SADDLE BROOK,

TORONTO

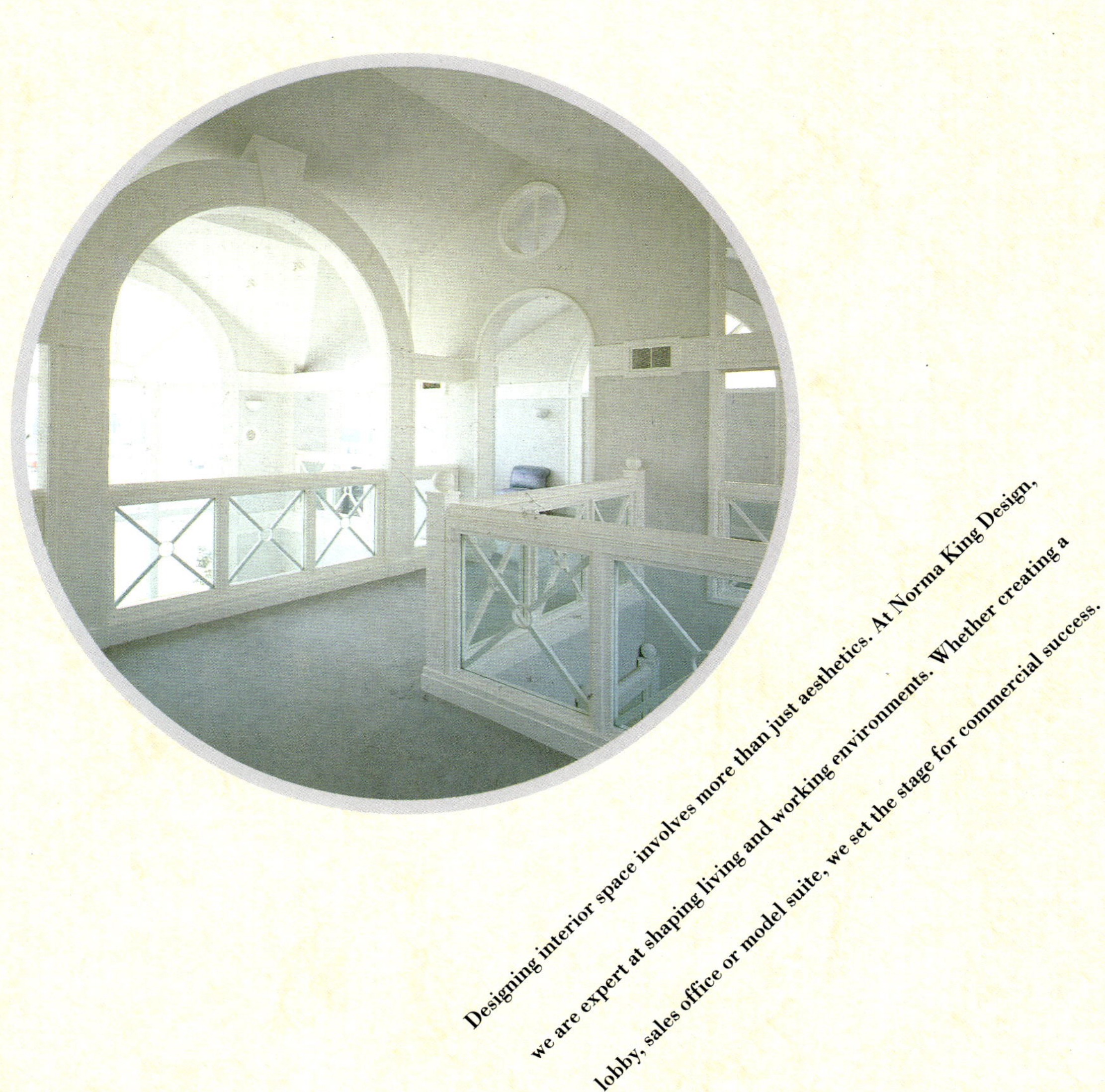

Designing interior space involves more than just aesthetics. At Norma King Design, we are expert at shaping living and working environments. Whether creating a lobby, sales office or model suite, we set the stage for commercial success.

LOBBY 60 E. 88 ST., NEW YORK

Interior design is the integration of many elements into a cohesive whole.

At Norma King Design, we are constantly searching for the perfect solution.

114a Sackville Street, Toronto, Ontario, Canada M5A 3E7, (416) 862-9180, Interior Design Forum 1

Design 2 Inc. Toronto

JOHN F. SALADINO, INC.
305 EAST 63 STREET
NEW YORK CITY 10021

PHOTOGRAPHY BY DURSTON SAYLOR

JOHN
SALA
DINO

SERVICES

MARK BORCHELT

Photographer

Studio D
938-D Eisenhower Ave.
Alexandria, VA 22304
03-751-2533

MARK BORCHELT

Photographer

Studio D

4938-D Eisenhower Ave.
Alexandria, VA 22304
703-751-2533

POINT *of* VIEW
ARCHITECTURAL • RENDERINGS
JEFFREY W. CURCIO • ARLINGTON VIRGINIA • 703 920 7472

• Interior Exterior
• Color Line Half-Tones
• Floor Plans Elevations
• Corporate Retail
• Residential Hospitality

WEBER DESIGN
705 KING STREET
ALEXANDRIA
VIRGINIA 22314

703.548.0003

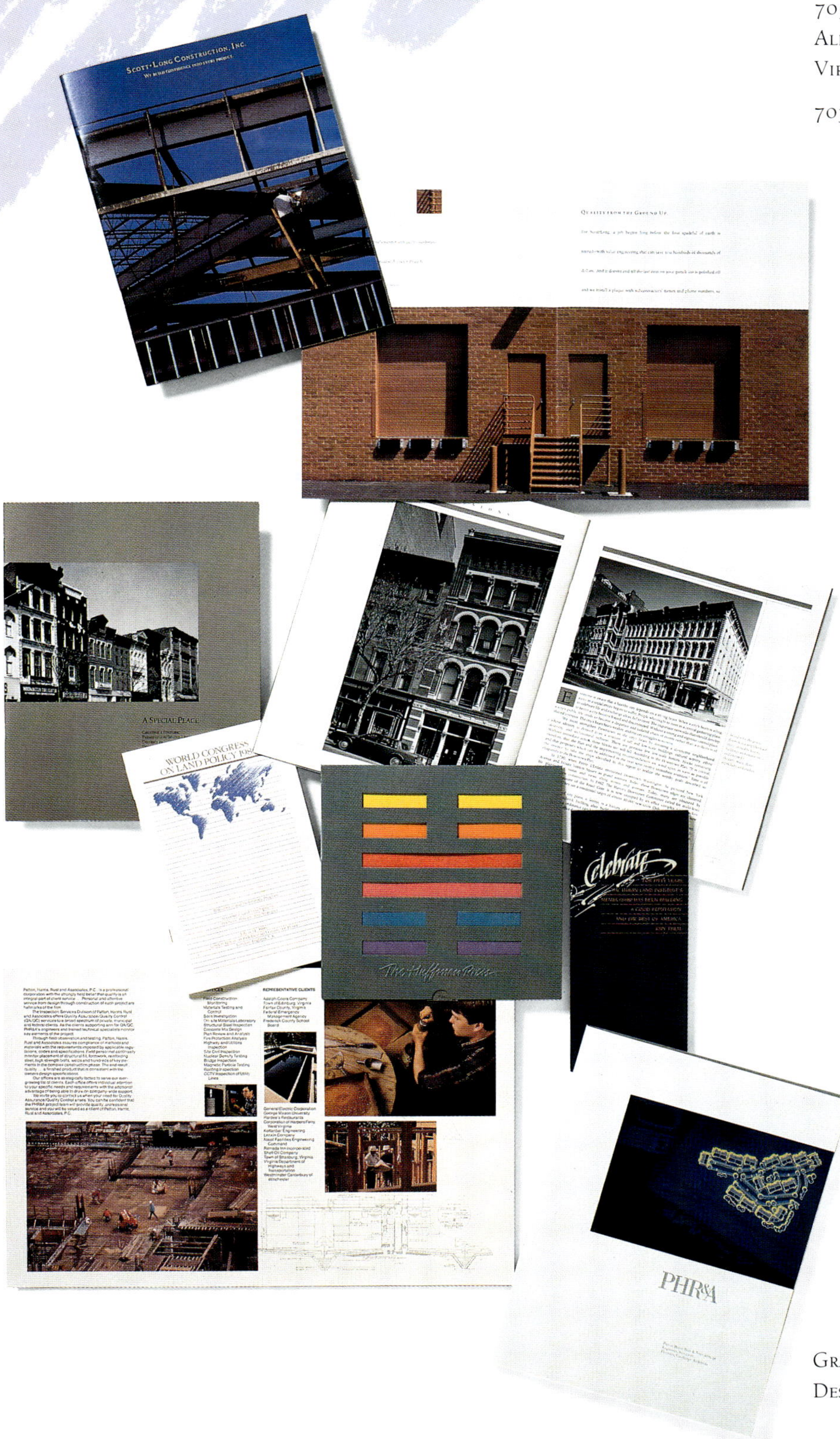

GRAPHIC
DESIGN

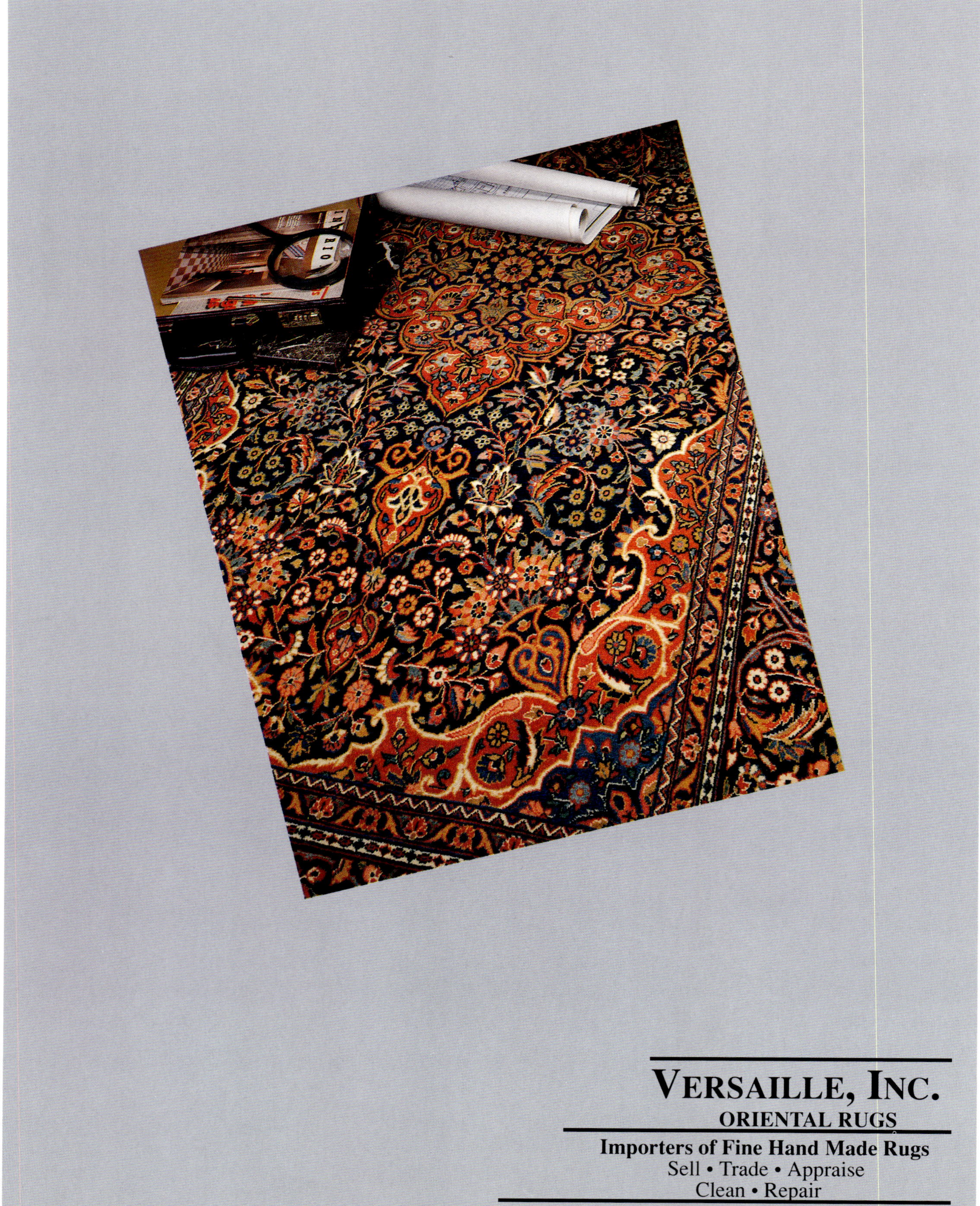
VERSAILLE, INC.
ORIENTAL RUGS
Importers of Fine Hand Made Rugs
Sell • Trade • Appraise
Clean • Repair
7101 Wisconsin Avenue • Bethesda, Maryland • (301) 657-3646

DESIGN
SCHOOLS

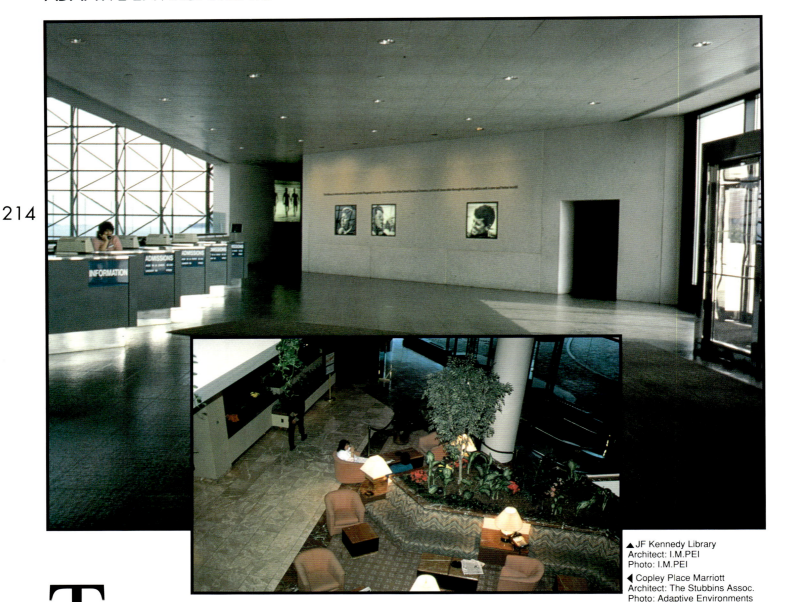

▲JF Kennedy Library
Architect: I.M.PEI
Photo: I.M.PEI

◀ Copley Place Marriott
Architect: The Stubbins Assoc.
Photo: Adaptive Environments

Thoughtful, timely inclusion of accessible design features in interior spaces result in environments which allow everyone to fully use them. Considering access at early stages in the design process will ensure the full integration of barrier free features with the rest of the design program. This is true for new construction as well as rehabilitation. High quality design work always incorporates accessibility as a principal design criterion.

Virtually all types of construction today needs to include elements of barrier free design. State and federal legislation, code regulations, and national standards require and set guidelines for architectural accessibility.

At any point in time as many as 50 million people are affected by temporary or chronic impairments which can make walking difficult or impossible; restrict one's ability to use standard door knobs; make it hard for visitors to orient themselves in a building and/or find rooms or offices or prevent a valued employee from returning to work after an injury. Our aging population is creating a growing number of people over the age of 60.

The effects of aging, alone, can create limitations of stamina, vision, hearing, and mobility which can be effectively responded to by interior designers. All working and living environments need to reflect the sometimes abruptly changing needs of those who use these places.

As designers and consultants to architects and developers, Adaptive Environments assures that accessibility is esthetically achieved. The best accessible design is that which goes unnoticed. Our projects include residential, commercial, institutional, historic, transportation facilities, office parks, hotels, municipal, and more. Facilities in Boston include Faneuil Hall Marketplace, South Station, Logan Airport, MBTA, 75 State Street; in Burlington, New England Executive Park, Burlington Mall.

621 Huntington Avenue
Boston, Massachusetts 02115

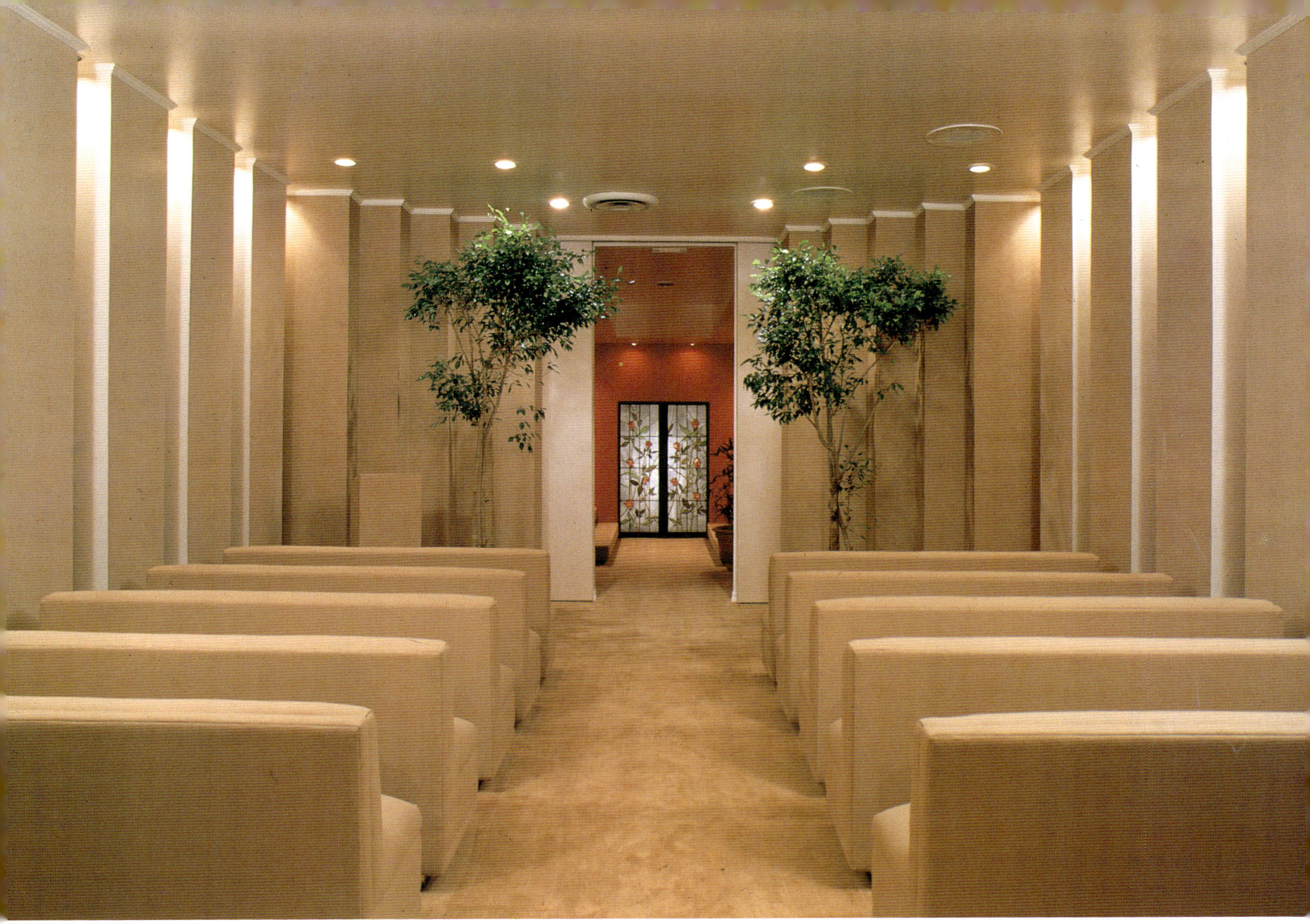

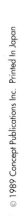

Photography: Dennis Krukowski
Graphic Design: Robert Coon

ROSEHILL MEMORIAL CHAPEL,
LINDEN, NEW JERSEY;
STUDENT PROJECT,
THOMAS HAUSER.

BERNARD LIPSCOMB
ASSOCIATE PROFESSIOR OF INTERIOR DESIGN AND FINE ARTS

Photography: Greg Kolp

THE CENTER FOR ADDICTIVE ILLNESSES,
MORRISTOWN, NEW JERSEY;
STUDENT PROJECT,
DEBRA TOSI, CLAIRE ROHLOFF.

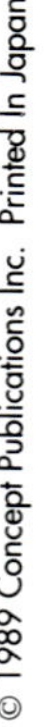

ENVIRONMENTAL DESIGN

Architecture

Interiors

Landscape

"I believe that an architecture/interiors/landscape education today must help students to take an expanded view of design, absorb the rich variety of new sources of artistic content which surround them today, and shape their own philosophies. This kind of experience is as much a training for the enjoyment of life as it is for professional practice."
JAMES WINES

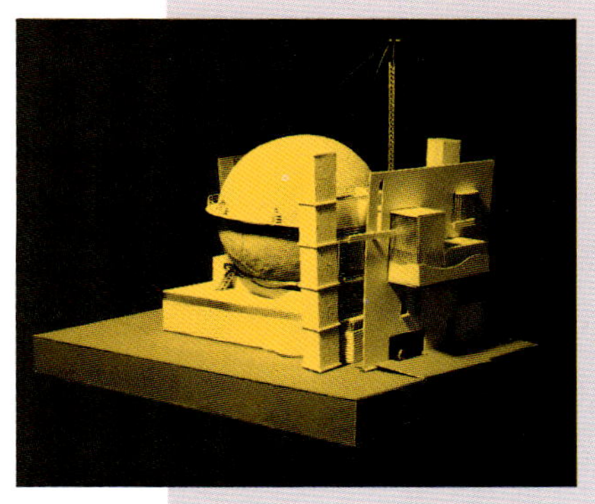

parsons school of design

"Environmental Design is about developing a design point of view—about having a position, a philosophy of design. The courses taught me to think spatially, to understand problem-solving through a design process, and to develop my own unique sensibility."
ANDREA McBRIDE
Class of '87, Designer

Parsons School of Design

Parsons School of Design, one of America's oldest and, today, its largest private college of the visual arts is, in fact, a system of schools encompassing three campuses, in New York City, Los Angeles and Paris. Because of its carefully coordinated curriculum, Parsons students have the unique opportunity to experience first hand the different cultural and professional orientations of these three world centers of art and design, and have the option of spending a year or more away from their "home" campus, without leaving the Parsons system.

The college, which offers undergraduate degrees in photography, painting, sculpture, illustration, fashion design, environmental design, craft/product design, and communication design, also has a broad-ranging graduate curriculum, leading to MFA and MA degrees in such unique disciplines as architectural lighting design, the history of the decorative arts, architectural and design criticism, painting, sculpture, and education. A two-year Master of Architecture is in its final planning stages, and it is expected that an innovative, 6-year, "4 + 2" BFA/M. Arch. sequence will be implemented shortly.

The first school in the United States to offer a formal curriculum in interior design, Parsons has long dominated this profession, and its alumni have had a profound influence on the field as it has come of age from the 1920s on. In the 1960s, this curriculum was drastically altered, and focussed its attention upon the designer's impact in the social arena, looking in particular at problems that placed significant pressure on the center city environment. Thus for the first time students and faculty, often working on model projects with government or private "clients," consistently addressed such issues as the design of jails, municipal hospitals, transportation systems, or storefront drug treatment centers and, in general, examined the needs of the urban infrastructure in an emerging socio/design crisis. During the 1970s, this orientation became increasingly focussed on issues that were properly defined within the realm of architecture itself, and the curriculum began to develop two distinct undergraduate options, the first based upon a rethinking the role of the interior designer in contemporary society—addressing the traditional issues of residential and commercial/contract design, but also examining the designer's impact on the social and political structure of urban life; and the second, a clearly defined "pre-architecture" track which incorporated the same social and philosophical emphasis.

Under the direction of James Wines, President and founder of SITE, who assumed the department's chairmanship in 1984, the program has continued to expand upon its pioneering work, examining the relevance of new ideas and design directions within the context of the design, technological, and social heritage of the 20th Century. These efforts have been substantially enhanced by Parsons' 1970 merger with The New School for Social Research, an urban university with a long and distinguished tradition at the forefront of investigation and curricular innovation in the world of social sciences, urban affairs, and policy analysis. The broad intellectual base provided by this vital and active community of scholars combines with the distinguished artists and designers who comprise the Parsons faculty, creating an academic setting whose creative energy may well be unmatched in any city of the world.

"The thing that is most remarkable about the Environmental Design program is the diversity of ideologies represented by the faculty. I think that this diversity is a 'personification' of the immense variety of New York City. The program helped me to understand why I want to become an architect, and introduced me to issues of design as a social art that I will think about for the rest of my life."
WILLIAM MASSIE
Class of '87, Designer

"Design is taught as an environmental phenomena where a conceptual strategy is developed for the entire project, where the interior is an extension of the architecture. The department provided me with a strong background in art, as well as important technical knowledge and skills; it has helped me as a designer and teacher to 'see' spatially and to understand that there must be a theoretical basis for all design. Environmental Design taught me a way of thinking."
ELIZABETH DUNCAN
Class of '85, Designer

Environmental Design:
Architecture, Interiors, Landscape

The Department of Environmental Design provides a Bachelor of Fine Arts degree program in contemporary design. The interdisciplinary curriculum focuses on the design, conditions, and theoretical ideas concerning architecture, interior space, and landscape. The objective of the curriculum is to encourage each student to develop individual creative interests and strategies through an emphasis on synthetic thinking about design as process and invention.

The first half of the three-year program provides students with a background and foundation in visual literacy, spatial thinking, abstract manipulation, and design anaylsis taught through a core of required courses in studio, history, technology, and fine arts. Following this progressive sequence of courses, students structure the remaining portion of their program. Elective studios and

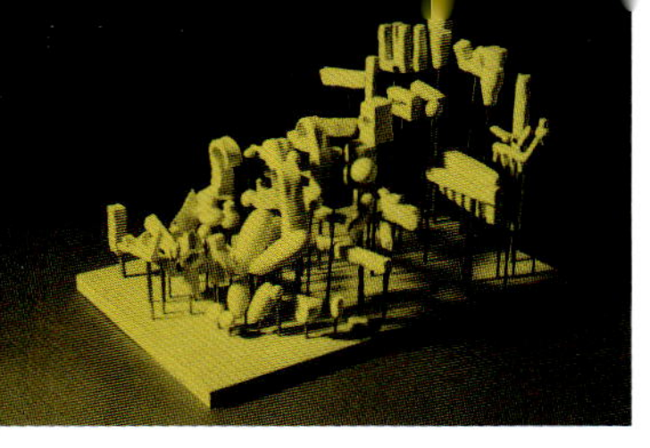

academic courses give students an opportunity to direct their creative work and pursue particular interests in architecture, interior design, and landscape design. While students are encouraged to focus their interests, the department does not encourage narrow specialization.

In the past ten years there has been a dramatic increase in the number of small design firms that offer a variety of services to clients (including architecture, interior, landscape, furniture, and graphic design). There is every indication that this is not a short-lived trend but a substantive change in the orientation of the design professions in the future. Students of Environmental Design are uniquely qualified to work in this new professional world because of their interdisciplinary education, their understanding of design at a range of scales and contexts, and the rigor of their training—intellectually, conceptually, technically, and visually. Parsons' department emphasizes this constructive synthesis as the best preparation for professional practice in all design fields.

The Environmental Design curriculum prepares students for productive careers, as well as providing a strong academic experience for those individuals who choose to continue their design studies in graduate programs at Parsons/New School or other institutions. Parsons School of Design offers related graduate programs in Lighting Design, the History of Decorative Arts, and Architecture and Design Criticism. A Master of Architecture program is currently in development.

Advantages of Studying Environmental Design at Parsons

• Parsons/New School has one of the best locations in Manhattan, offering students all the benefits of New York City's vast cultural resources.

• The college attracts a teaching staff of America's leading designers who are active in the disciplines taught.

• As a result of Parsons' divisional structure within The New School, a university with an active graduate division devoted to urban issues (The Graduate School of Management) with a distinguished Graduate school in the social sciences as well, each student can combine design education with superior academic resources.

Unique Aspects of the Program

• The curriculum is oriented toward architecture, interior design, and landscape design, taught from the standpoint of visual art.

• The program encourages interdisciplinary participation in design, with an emphasis on helping the student see the value of developing a personal philosophy. The decreasing need for traditional specialization and demand for knowledge in multiple areas mean that a graduate of this integrated design program is better prepared for current professional practice.

• By having a faculty drawn from active professional life, students gain early insights that help them with design problems, business organization, future employment and the selection of graduate education.

• Beginning with a strong foundation in the understanding of architectural space and structural problems, students are then encouraged to focus their work more specifically in the junior year.

• Students in the department are offered mobility programs in Paris and in Los Angeles. In addition there are graduate programs in decorative arts, lighting design, and architecture and design criticism. Currently under development, there will be a graduate architectural program for Fall of 1989, offering a professional degree.

• A dynamic lecture and conference program gives students access to these leading personalities through public and in-studio dialogues. Past visitors have included Robert Venturi, Denise Scott Brown, Tom Wolfe, Peter Cook, Coop Himmelblau, Peter Eisenman, Zaha Hadid, Bernard Tschumi, Francesco Dal Co, Michael Sorkin, Charles Jencks, Charles Gandee, Joe D'urso, Michael Kalil, and others.

Professional And Educational Options After Graduation

• Students are prepared to work for professional organizations in the fields of architecture, interior design, and landscape design. Because of Environmental Design's interdisciplinary concept of education, graduates have also entered such professions as graphics, jewlery making, film making, rendering and model building, lighting design, arts administration, design marketing, design administration, and urban planning.

• Students may choose from the graduate program offered by Parsons or seek graduate degrees at other institutions. Environmental Design graduates have been accepted at all leading architectural schools.

"I think that the experimental nature of the design studios at Parsons is very significant. It encourages students to develop a critical stance, a theory and philosophy of design. The courses and studios were stimulating; part of this has to do with being in New York, but also because there is a broad range of students. All of this makes the program very enriching and very unusual."
ROBERT WELBORN
Class of '87, Freelance Designer

"Environmental Design at Parsons prepared me for a career in architecture, as well as the limitless variety of alternative creative activities. It was an education that was expansive—not limiting."
MERYL WAITZ
Class of '85, Jewelry Designer

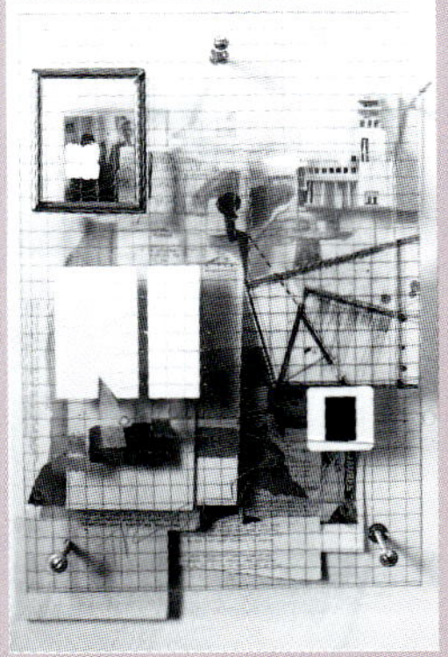

For more information on Environmental Design at Parsons School of Design, please contact:
Environmental Design
Parsons School of Design
66 Fifth Avenue
New York, NY 10011
212-741-8955

The faculty of Environmental Design is an exceptional group of teachers who are also highly regarded designers and professionals in their fields. Their active and creative involvement in the design community provides a network for students for professional advisement and future employment.

Faculty

James Wines, Chairman
Patricia C. Phillips, Associate Chairman
Karen Bausman
Stephanie Bower
Susan Bower
Constantin Boym
Christopher Compton
Maria Conelli
Suzan Courtney
Elizabeth English
Leslie Gill
Steven Holt
Archie Kaplan
Laszlo Kiss
Kunio Kudo
Sanford Kwinter
Andrew MacNair
Nancy Manter
Anton Martinez
Robert McAnulty
Michael McDonough
Shauna Mosseri
John Nambu
Mark Robbins
Lee Stout
Anthony Tsirantonakis
Allan Wexler
Peter Wheelwright
Carol Willis
Todd Zwigard

Design: Alisa Rashish, NYC

JAMES WINES
"I believe that an architecture/interiors/landscape education today must help students to take an expanded view of design, absorb the rich variety of new sources of artistic content which surround them today, and shape their own philosophies. This kind of experience is as much a training for the enjoyment of life as it is for professional practice."

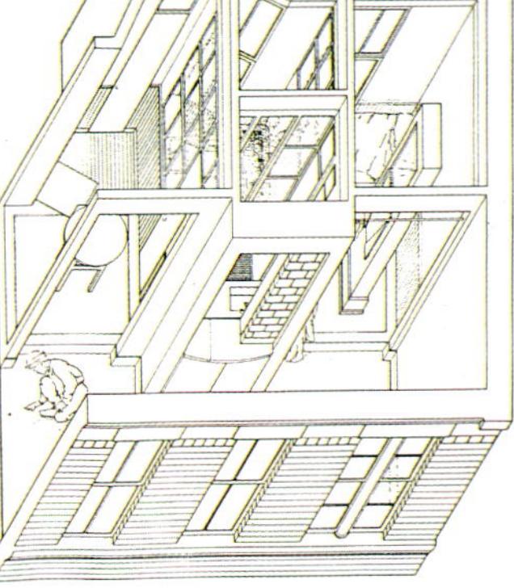

MARK ROBBINS
"My bias is towards an architecture that is inclusive. It affects and is affected by the arts and culture of its time. To study it and the process of its making isolated from this context avoids a significant level of meaning . . . An educator, as I see it, should be able to guide a student through his or her own choices in the design process and foster a consciousness of the individual's motivation and responsibility."

STEVEN HOLT
"I favor clarity and chaos, simplicity and contradiction, directness and ambiguity. I believe architecture and design are public art forms and should incorporate figurative as well as literal imagery. I believe that when opposites collide, interesting things happen."

ALLAN WEXLER
"Qualities that I look for and encourage in a student . . . A student who wants to attain a balance between the logical and illogical, a student who takes risks, a student who loves to work, a student who loves to play, a student who wants to see the students around him/her do well, a student who doesn't want to do what I do, a student who wants to know what I do."

MICHAEL McDONOUGH
"The goal of any educational program should be students who know how to ask questions, both of themselves and their environment. This is the beginning of wisdom.
To be an artist, a creative individual, requires both tremendous discipline and the courage to be completely honest. Education is not about training acolytes; it is about training dissidents."

SHAUNA MOSSERI
"Teaching is a reciprocal activity. It consists simultaneously of offering to the student an established body of knowledge and eliciting from the student his own understanding of the world drawn from intuition and experience."

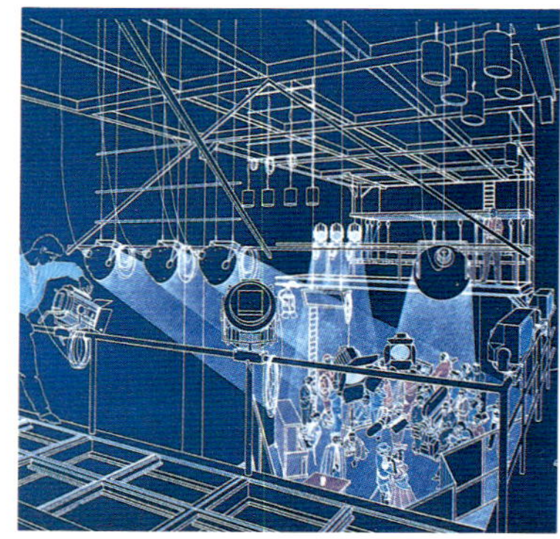

ANDREW MacNAIR
"Design education involves the dual operations of research along with design projects. The aim is to generate proposed projections for a new design that acts as a critique of current, stale dogma."

PETER WHEELWRIGHT
"It is essential for understanding architecture or any form of environmental design to consider that there are no new spaces and forms. There are only new meanings. These possible meanings are latent in the program and allow us, as architects/designers, to be responsive beyond the overwrought issues of style."

KAREN BAUSMAN/LESLIE GILL
"As educators, our fundamental responsibility is to draw out and help develop the mental powers of another—teaching a student HOW to think, not WHAT to think."

The three Pratt Institute alumni whose work appears here share a common trait: the Pratt Edge, an understanding of interior design that gives them an important edge over their competitors.

Pratt's interior design program covers all aspects of interior design, beginning with the fundamentals of drawing right through to the complexities of building construction, architectural drawing, computer graphics, professional practice, and contract administration.

At Pratt, your studies are supported by an entire design school as well as a School of Liberal Arts and Sciences, to give you a background not only in interior design, but also in the history of art, design and the world around you.

Additionally, Pratt's network of faculty, alumni, and friends, coupled with its New York City location, will put you at the center of the design world. Pratt is able to draw on the best interior design talent available, including the three alumni shown here, all of whom teach at the Institute.

At Pratt, in an undergraduate or graduate program in interior design, you'll learn what gave these alumni—and hundreds more like them—the Pratt Edge.

Gustav W. Rohrs, Chairperson
Department of Interior Design

FOR INFORMATION

Pratt Institute offers a Bachelor of Fine Arts degree and a Master of Science degree in Interior Design. The undergraduate program is a four-year course of study that gives students a complete background in interior design. The graduate program requires the completion of a minimum of 48 credits. For graduate students without interior design backgrounds, Pratt offers a qualifying program. For more information, contact Gus Rohrs at Pratt Institute (718) 636-3630 or the Pratt Admissions Office, (718) 636-3669 or write to Pratt at 200 Willoughby Avenue, Brooklyn, NY 11205.

MYONGGI SUL

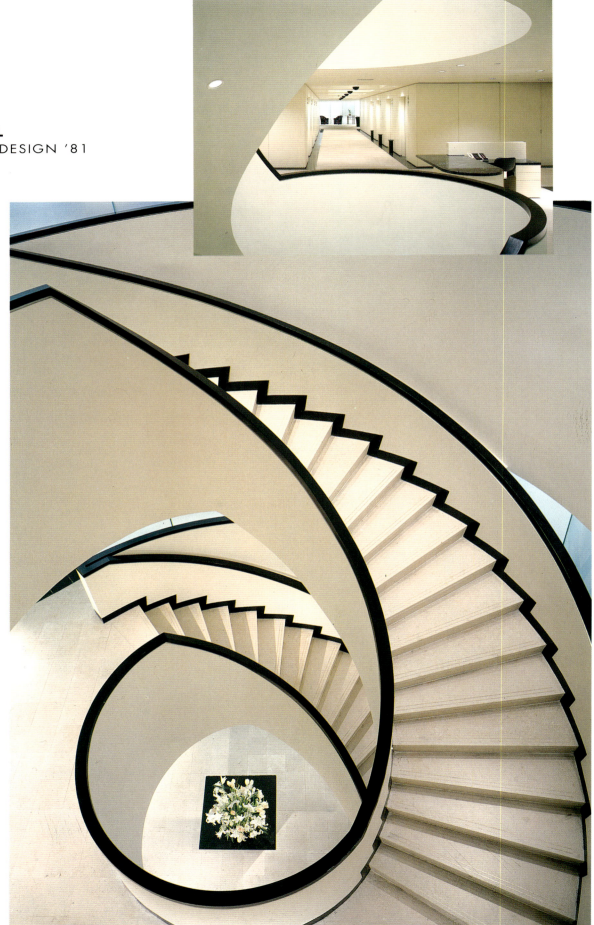

M.S., INTERIOR DESIGN '81

Myonggi Sul is a senior designer and associate with GN Associates with major responsibilities for client contact, programming, schematic, and design development.

The work shown was done for the J.P. Stevens showrooms and offices in Manhattan. The flooring materials, polished black granite and bush hammered limestone, begin to define the vocabulary of the public street. The primary showing area on the 12th floor is entered via the sweeping circular stair and is developed as a series of individual storefronts with interchangeable displays. The result is a visually striking environment that meets the needs of dynamic marketing organization.

Myonggi Sul teaches color and materials in the Graduate Interior Design Department.

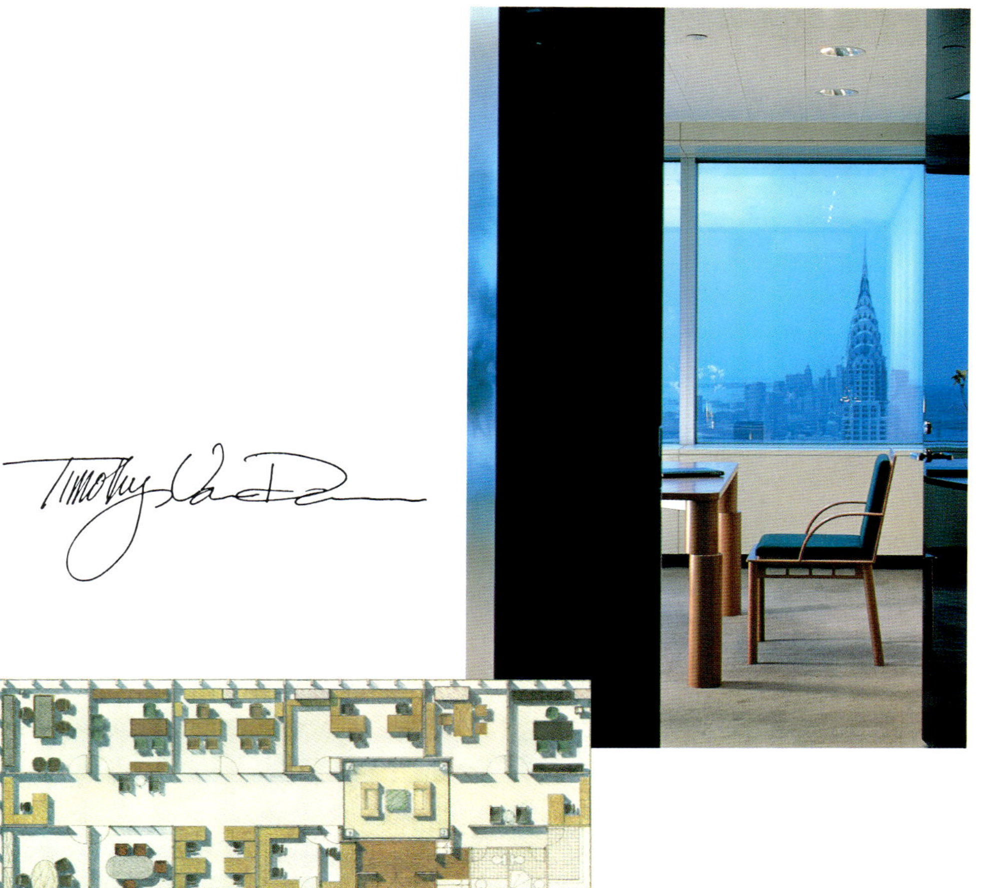

TIM VAN DAM

M.S., INTERIOR DESIGN, '78

Tim Van Dam opened his own design office in1986 after a career that included stints with Knoll International and Hertzfeld/Carder Design.

For the offices of Knoll International Holdings, designed in collaboration with two other designers, he has created a showcase for Knoll products, including furniture, wall partitions, textiles, and carpet. "We created a 'main street' through the center of the space, delineated with full height, using frosted glass panels terminating at the window wall. This allows the maximum of natural light to reach the support staff while meeting the requirement for executive offices with full privacy."

Tim Van Dam joined the faculty of Pratt Institute's Graduate Interior Design Program in1986.

RON WAGNER

B.F.A., INTERIOR DESIGN '75

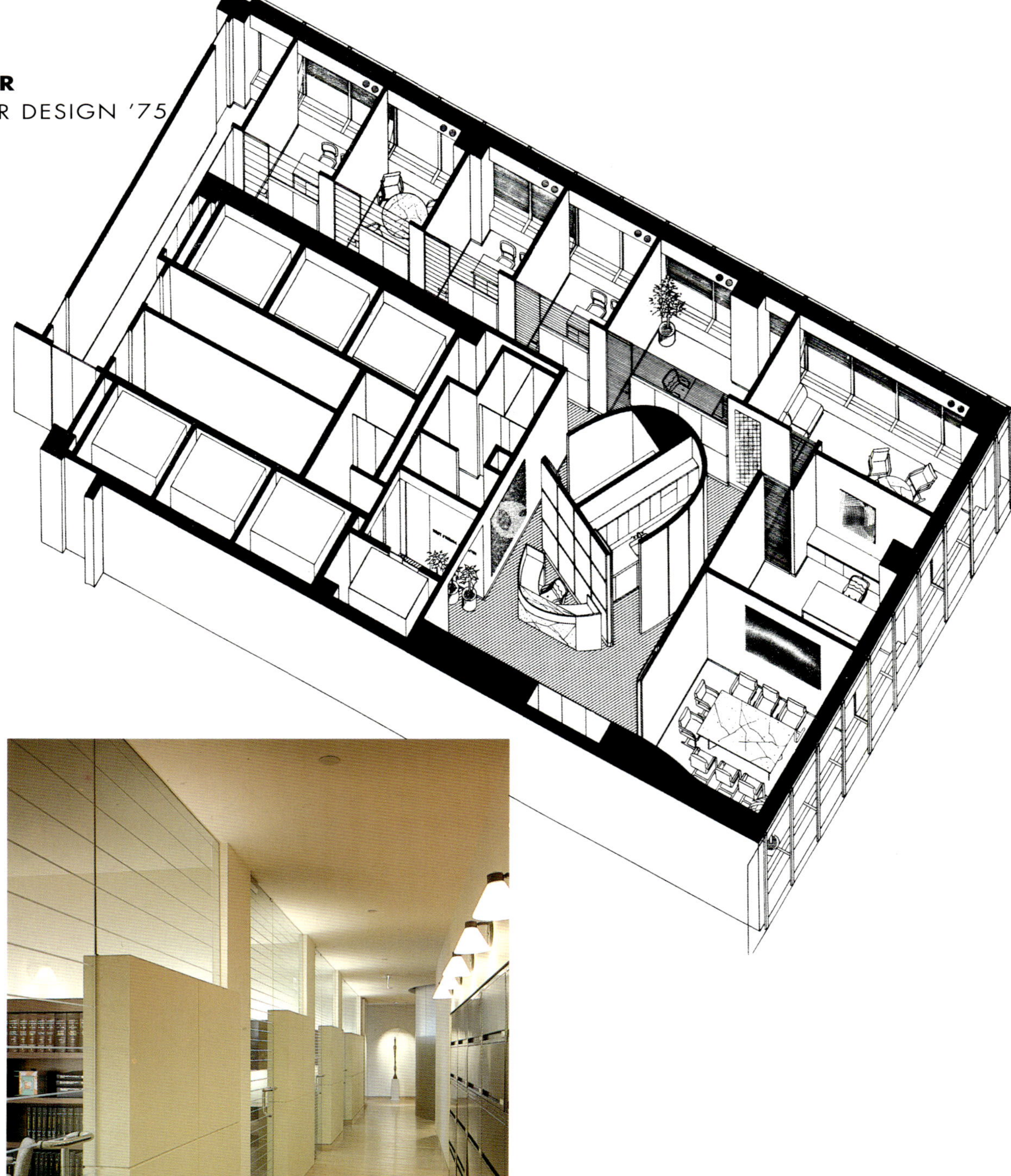

Ron Wagner is a principal of Ron Wagner Design, a firm whose annual volume of work is approximately $1 million.

The work shown is office space for Riker, Danzig, Scherer, Hyland & Perretti, New Jersey's largest law firm. "A sense of natural light and public access to the incredible views of the designer and the client. Our plan consists of a ring of perimeter offices punctuated by a wood and glass grid enclosing conference rooms at opposite ends of the elevator lobby."

For First Sterling Corporation, Ron Wagner worked in collaboration with another designer to create space for his midtown Manhattan real estate investment firm. "The concept was to provide individual private offices while allowing natural light into the public space. The finishes are light neutral colors to enhance the sense of openness."

Ron Wagner is a visiting associate professor at Pratt Institute, teaching undergraduate design courses.

Ron Wagner

AWARDS

Project: Celeste Bartos Forum
Client: The New York Public Library
Architects: Davis, Brody & Associates

Project: Majestic Theatre
Client: Brooklyn Academy of Music
Architects: Hardy, Holzman, Pfeiffer

Project:	548 West 22nd Street
Client:	DIA Art Foundation
Architect:	Richard Gluckman

Townhouse For A Single Titania

The owner longs to one day raise a family in this townhouse in Greenwhich Village. Today she is content to spin her life as one, in a set of formal rooms on the lower floors.

She is a sensual woman with specific affinities which map her character: The Renaissance as described by Giotto and Piero della Francesca; Paris through the eyes of Madame and Cocteau in the fifties; religious and cultural rituals as perceived through foreign eyes; Flemish light frozen by Vermeer.

She is a private woman with resurging personal memories which chart her inner realm: Light shifting against glistening surfaces making them seem at once cool and hot; mosquito netting shrouding the bed; small places in which to hide; vast surfaces on which to dance.

These disparate perceptions and moods are unified by one element, which is this person, who has found a soulful link between them.

The architect's homage to her, therefore, is to construct an architecture as sonnet, an ode to these fascinating fascinations.

BEDROOM, first floor

BEDROOM FIREPLACE, first floor

• LIVING ROOM, first floor

• BATHROOM, first floor

• MEDITATION ROOM, first floor

• DINING ROOM, garden floor

• BEDROOM VANITY, first floor

DEN, second floor

DUPONT

A N T R O N®

CARPET OF ANTRON PRECEDENT® BRINGS MAINTENANCE COSTS DOWN TO EARTH.

The wrong carpet can turn out to be your worst enemy. Its looks quickly begin to fade, your cleaning bills soar. But not with Antron Precedent® That's because Antron Precedent® resists soiling and stains better than any other commercial carpet.

So you can enjoy lower maintenance costs. And, because it keeps its texture longer, the beauty lasts up to twice as long as many other carpets. Beauty, durability and lower maintenance costs. No wonder people are falling for Antron Precedent®

For more information, call 1-800-448-9835.

THE ANSWERS COME EASY WITH ANTRON®

DuPont Design Consultants In The Mid-Atlantic Region

Philadelphia, Delaware
Southern New Jersey

Catherine Lownes
(215) 836-9429

Baltimore, Washington, D.C.
Virginia

Susan Feild
(301) 557-7601

Atlanta, Southeast

Faith Brooks
(404) 963-2334

A great "quick response" program should blow you away.

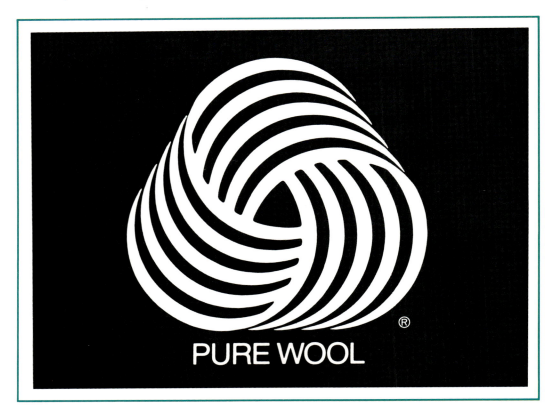